CYCLING

Lee N. Burkett/Paul W. Darst

Charles B. Corbin/Philip E. Allsen, Series Editors

SPORT FOR LIFE

BOWLING	Joyce M. Harrison *Brigham Young University* Ron Maxey
CYCLING	Lee N. Burkett Paul W. Darst *Arizona State University*
JOGGING	David E. Corbin *The University of Nebraska at Omaha*
RACQUETBALL	Robert P. Pangrazi *Arizona State University*
STRENGTH TRAINING *Beginners, Bodybuilders, and Athletes*	Philip E. Allsen *Brigham Young University*

Charles B. Corbin/Philip E. Allsen, Series Editors

SPORT FOR LIFE

CYCLING

Lee N. Burkett
Paul W. Darst
Arizona State University

Charles B. Corbin/Philip E. Allsen, Series Editors

Scott, Foresman and Company
Glenview, Illinois   London

Cover photograph by Robert Drea

Library of Congress Cataloging-in-Publication Data

Burkett, Lee N.
   Cycling.

   (Sport for life series)
   Bibliography: p. 146
   Includes index.
   1. Cycling.   I. Darst, Paul W.   II. Title.
III. Series.
GV1041.B78   1987   796.6   86-29765
ISBN 0-673-18357-2

1 2 3 4 5 6 7-MVN-92 91 90 89 88 87

Foreword

We are calling this series SPORT FOR LIFE because we believe a sports skills series should be more than just a presentation of the "rules of the game." A popular sport or activity should be presented in a way that encourages understanding through direct experience, improvement through prompt correction, and enjoyment through proper mental attitude.

Over the years, each SPORT FOR LIFE author has instructed thousands of people in their selected activity. We are delighted these "master teachers" have agreed to put down in writing the concepts and procedures they have developed successfully in teaching a skill.

The books in the SPORT FOR LIFE series present other unique features as appropriate to the featured sport or activity.

The Sport Experience: This is a learning activity that explains and teaches a technique or specific rule. Whether it requires the reader to experience selecting a specific bicycle, stroking a backhand in tennis, or choosing an approach to use in bowling it carries the learner right to the heart of the game or activity at a pace matching his or her own progress. The Sport Experience is identified throughout the book with its own special typographical design.

The Error Corrector: The SPORT FOR LIFE authors have taken specific skills and listed some of the common errors encountered by participants; at the same time they have listed the methods to be utilized to correct these errors. The Error Corrector can be compared to a road map as it provides checkpoints toward skillful performance of a sport or activity.

The Mental Game: Understanding the mental game can remove many of the obstacles to success. The authors have devised techniques to aid the reader in planning playing strategy and in learning how to cope with the stress of competition. It is just as important to know how to remove mental errors as it is to deal with the physical ones.

The editors and authors of SPORT FOR LIFE trust that their approach and enthusiasm will have a lasting effect on each reader and will help promote a lifetime of health and happiness, physically and psychologically, for a sport well played or an activity well performed.

Charles B. Corbin/Philip E. Allsen

About the Authors and Editors

Lee N. Burkett and Paul W. Darst. Drs. Burkett and Darst are fellow faculty members in the Department of Health and Physical Education at Arizona State University, Tempe Arizona. Both are active in their profession and serve on numerous editorial boards for journals concerned with physical education, recreation, and sports medicine. Dr. Darst is co-author of books on physical education in the high school and on outdoor activities and recreation.

Charles B. Corbin. Dr. Corbin is Professor of Physical Education at Arizona State University. A widely known expert on fitness and health, he is author or co-author of 27 books addressed to students on those topics ranging from the elementary school through college. In August, 1986, he was given the "Better Health and Living Award" by that magazine as one of ten Americans who have made the difference in influencing others in the areas of health and fitness. He is a 1982 recipient of the National Honor Award from the American Alliance for Health, Physical Education, Recreation and Dance and is a fellow in the American Academy of Physical Education.

Philip E. Allsen. Dr. Allsen is Professor of Physical Education and Director of the Fitness for Life Program at Brigham Young University in Provo, Utah. Widely known for his expertise in physical fitness, sports medicine, and athletic training, Dr. Allsen, a prolific writer, has authored more than 75 articles and written six books covering the topics of strength and physical fitness. The "Fitness for Life" program, which Dr. Allsen developed at Brigham Young University, now serves approximately 7,000 students at the institution each year and has been adopted by more than 400 schools in the United States. He is a member of the American College of Sports Medicine, the American Alliance of Health, Physical Education, Recreation and Dance, and the National Collegiate Physical Education Association.

Preface

For many years, cycling has been an enjoyable experience for us. The time spent on our bicycles has given us the opportunity to enjoy the outdoors and relax from the busy lifestyles that we lead. We have enjoyed many benefits from riding and maintaining bicycles. Writing this book has given us the opportunity to share our knowledge and positive experiences with many others. With the many new bicycles on the market, the opportunities for exploring, commuting, and sightseeing on a bicycle are endless. A person of any age or ability level can have a successful experience on a bicycle. Cycling is an activity that you can enjoy and this book will help expedite the learning process.

We would like to offer special thanks to Professor Ginny Atkins, California State University, Fresno, for her extensive review of the manuscript. Her expert background in cycling and teaching experience in this area provided us with many suggestions and insights that have improved the book. Special thanks also needs to be extended to Professor Charles B. Corbin, Arizona State University, for his support and ideas on this project. The format of this book is the result of his thoughts and ideas on learning physical skills. Yvonne Morrison, a cycling instructor at Arizona State University was also helpful with photos and additional information. A final thanks is also extended to our families for their support and encouragement throughout the process.

We hope that you will find joy and success with many cycling activities. Best wishes for a positive experience with cycling. Make it a part of your lifestyle.

Lee N. Burkett
Paul W. Darst

Contents

How to Begin

Congratulations on deciding to become a cyclist! Bicycling can be an exciting activity. In this book a wealth of information and enjoyable activities are made available to you. Cycling is a great lifetime activity that can be fun for all people regardless of age or physical ability. Young and old alike can enjoy the challenge and stimulation of bicycling activities. Cycling is a great activity for the disabled as well as the highly skilled. The bike can be used for transportation, for physical fitness, for exploring, for camping, for racing, for relaxing, and for many other reasons. Cycling can be done alone to get away from other problems, or it can be done with a group to enjoy the company of others. It can be a family affair (see Figure 1.1) for all members from 4 years to 84 years, or it can be a husband and wife activity to get away from the children for a short while.

There are many benefits to becoming a regular bicycle rider. The necessary skills are relatively simple to master. In comparison to many other physical activities, you need only minimal amounts of practice to attain the necessary skills. We are happy to welcome you to the growing number of bicycle enthusiasts. We hope to motivate you and improve your knowledge and skills so that you can enjoy cycling for the rest of your life. We believe that the process of learning a new physical activity should be an enjoyable adventure and that new participants should feel good about themselves during this process. After finishing this book, we hope you are attracted to cycling and will desire to be a cyclist forever!

Figure 1.1   Family outing on bicycles

UNIQUE SPORT FOR LIFE FEATURES

This SPORT FOR LIFE book is unique in that it is arranged with many hands-on types of learning activities in each chapter. These activities are arranged from the simplest to the most complex. You should be able to find success quickly with the early activities and then progress to more challenging activities throughout each chapter. You should keep in mind that all people regardless of ability will be able to find success with these activities. It may take some people a little longer than others to accomplish some of the particular skills, but that should not be a problem because you have a lifetime to enjoy bicycling. We have tried to take nothing for granted regarding the knowledge and skills of our readers. Our system of activities called "The Sport Experience" should provide you with the motivation and confidence necessary to enjoy biking. You should be able to follow these activities and, with practice and patience, become as good as you want to become.

The book starts at the beginning level and takes you through a series of varied activities that will take you into intermediate and some advanced level skills. It is not a high technology book requiring you to purchase expensive equipment nor is it a book on bicycle racing. It is a beginning level book that is geared to beginning recreational riders who want to make biking a part of their lifestyle. The experience of the authors is focused on riding for fun, riding to work, and riding for exercise and fitness. We have tried to promote a simple, success-oriented process and have avoided making everything so complex that it scares beginners away from trying many of the skills. There are a variety of bicycling activities in this book that all people should be able to enjoy as they progress with their riding skills.

Chapter 1 includes information on getting started and the various benefits of bicycling. The second chapter focuses on the extensive range of equipment and accessories that can be selected by the beginner. The third chapter provides many suggestions for using your bicycle and ways of incorporating bicycling into your lifestyle, as well as many activities for developing the range of skills that will help you to use your bicycle effectively. Chapter 4 provides many safety ideas and activities that will help you to become a safe bicyclist. Bicycle maintenance is the topic of activities for Chapter 5. It will take you through the simplest activities of changing a tire to the complex process of repacking the bearings in the bottom bracket. The final chapter is entitled "Going Beyond—Possibilities for the Future" because it provides you with information on several advanced options available to you and your bicycle. There are several advanced cycling activities and opportunities that you may enjoy after you have been cycling a while. A little information and practice can prepare you for most of these activities.

WARM-UP AND PRECONDITIONING

Bicycling is an activity that does not require a specific warm-up procedure (except for racing). In almost all situations, it is appropriate to just get on your bike and start slowly enough to warm yourself up while on the bicycle. Bicycling is not usually vigorous enough to require a specific warm-up procedure. Warming up is necessary if you are going to be pedaling very fast as soon as you get on the bike. For example, if you eventually become a bicycle racer, you will want to develop a warm-up routine to prepare for the vigorous race. Otherwise, we recommend that you start each ride slowly enough to allow the body to gradually warm up.

As far as a specific preconditioning program that will prepare you to become a better cyclist, we are assuming that you are a beginner who has not been involved in a regular physical activity program. We think that it is perfectly appropriate to go ahead and begin riding the bike slowly. Do not try any long rides or steep hills until you improve your physical fitness. It is important to understand that you are going to have to start slowly and realize that you may have some initial muscular soreness. This soreness is caused by the specificity of the activity and a lack of muscular endurance. You will probably have some soreness in your hands, arms, legs, back of the neck, and your backside from the bicycle seat. This is all quite common for beginners. If the soreness persists for two or more days, you probably have overdone the activity and need to proceed at a slower pace. Remember that you have the rest of your life to enjoy your bicycle. Do not go too fast and injure yourself or burn yourself out by proceeding too quickly.

Basically, beginners need to condition their heart and vascular systems with many aerobic-type activities such as walking, jogging, and stair-climbing. Start slowly and keep track of the time, distance, and frequency of your preconditioning activities (see Chapter 3 for specific ideas).

These stretching and flexibility exercises are all specific to the muscle groups that you will be using during your bicycling activities. You can do all of these every other day or half of them one day and the other half the next day. You should use these in conjunction with your bicycling program as you begin developing your skills. These are beginning stretching activities, so remember to go slowly. If you have been relatively inactive for many years, it will take the body a little time to adjust to the increased demands. Remember that there is no hurry. As you become ready for more challenging conditioning programs, then check the various levels of conditioning programs that are available in Chapter 6 and Appendix A.

EQUIPMENT AND ACCESSORIES

The equipment and accessories for bicycling are extensive. New equipment is developed all the time sparked by modern technology. Bicycles are improved each year and it is fun to keep up with all that is available. The purchase of a bicycle is an especially important decision for a beginner because you must consider the types of bicycling that you intend on doing and all the options that are available in your price range. We have included a discussion on equipment options and several learning activities in Chapter 2. After reading the chapter and completing the learning activities, you should be ready to purchase a bicycle and the necessary equipment.

Simple stretching and flexibility exercises before and after cycling may help prevent soreness in the lower back and legs. Perform these stretches in a slow, static manner without any bouncing motion. Start slowly and do not stretch too hard. These stretches should be performed about every other day.

1. *Hamstrings and lower back:* From a standing position, bend forward and let your arms and head hang down while keeping the legs slightly flexed. Hold for a count of 15–20 seconds.
2. *Quadricep and knee:* From a standing position, grab the front of your ankle and pull the heel up toward the buttocks. You can place your other arm against a wall for support and balance. Be careful not to arch the back during the process. Do each leg hold for 15–20 seconds.
3. *Groin and hamstrings:* From a standing position, place one leg forward at about chest height on a secure object. The top leg should be flexed and pointed straight ahead. Lean forward slowly until you feel the stretch. Alternate both legs in the top position, holding each stretch for 15–20 seconds.
4. *Calf:* Stand about two feet away from a wall and lean forward toward the wall while keeping the feet and heels on the ground. Hold the position for 15 seconds and feel the stretch in the calf. You can vary this by putting one foot forward and leaning toward the wall.
5. *Lower back and groin:* Lie flat on your back and pull one knee up to the chest and hold that position for a 15 second count. Switch legs and repeat.
6. *Neck and upper back:* From the position of lying flat on your back with the knees flexed, put your hands behind your head and gently pull the head and upper back off the floor. Hold for 15 seconds.
7. *Back and hips:* From a sitting position, keep one leg straight and place the other leg in a bent position over the top of the straight leg with the foot outside the opposite knee. Twist the trunk and upper body toward the

Figure 1.2 Back and hips stretch

Figure 1.3 Squat position stretch for the groin

bent leg side until the elbow is hooked just above the knee (see Figure 1.2). Hold for a count of 15 seconds and repeat on the other side.

8. *Hamstrings:* From a sitting position, spread the legs apart about two feet and slowly bend forward at the hips toward one foot. Try to put your chin on your knee and hands on the ankle. Hold this position for 15 seconds and switch legs. Try the same exercise with the legs together.

9. *Groin and hips:* From a sitting position, place the soles of the feet together and pull the feet in toward the body.

Lean forward as far as possible from the hips and hold for 15 seconds.

10. *Ankles:* From a sitting position, lift up one leg and rotate the foot at the ankle to loosen and stretch the ankle. Switch legs and rotate the opposite ankle.

11. *Neck and shoulders:* Rotate the head in a circle around the neck both clockwise and counterclockwise. Shrug the shoulders upwards 5–10 times.

12. *Shoulders and arms:* Raise the arms up parallel to the ground and do 10 giant arm circles forward and backward. Switch the palms from a facing-down position to a facing-up position during the process.

13. *Groin, lower back, and legs:* Squat down with the feet about shoulder width and toes pointed slightly outward. Place the hands together and elbows inside the knees (see Figure 1.3). Gently apply pressure with the hands and elbows outward and hold for 15 seconds.

14. *Fingers and wrists:* Rotate the hands in a circular motion around the wrists both clockwise and counterclockwise. At the same time, open and close the fingers into a fist position.

BENEFITS OF BICYCLING

The benefits of bicycling fall into the areas of physiological, psychological, and financial. Bicycling is also an enjoyable form of play. These benefits are directly related to the types of bicycling that you do regularly and the attitude that you take into the activity. For example, there is little physiological gain if you only bicycle once a week for a short period of time. There is little financial gain unless you ride to work and use the bike in place of the automobile. Little psychological gain will occur if you are afraid of being run down by cars and trucks on a busy street while you are riding. Bicycling just to lose weight or improve the cardiovascular system will not be a form of play. If you do not truly enjoy cycling it may be difficult to maintain motivation for long periods of time. If you have decided to bicycle for specific benefits, then you need to make sure that you are doing the right kind of bicycling for the right amounts of time, intensity, and frequency. Many people have misconceptions about the ways to acquire certain benefits. We think that the enjoyable aspect of play is the most important benefit of cycling. People will persist at an activity longer if the process is enjoyable and provides them with an intrinsic type of satisfaction. There is certainly nothing wrong with the other benefits mentioned, but the play aspect will probably be the best motivator for most people.

Physiological Benefits

There are many physiological benefits from biking that have been well documented in the scientific literature. Bicycling at 5.5 miles per hour burns approximately five calories per minute or 300 calories per hour. Bicycling at thirteen miles per hour will burn more calories, approximately twelve calories per minute. Caloric expenditure combined with proper caloric intake can have a significant impact on weight control. Bicycling can improve the cardiovascular system, improve respiration, pulmonary capacity, and the amount of blood delivered with each stroke of the heart. Ken Cooper's popular aerobics plan for developing physical fitness awards five points for cycling five miles in less than twenty minutes. His program requires that thirty points be accumulated each week in order to develop and maintain a high level of fitness.

Figure 1.4   Riding a stationary bicycle for fitness

Good aerobic activity is useful in the reduction of cholesterol and blood fat levels. Since cycling is a good aerobic activity, it has these benefits. Cycling will also strengthen muscles, improve muscle tone, and improve muscular endurance. Arthritics have found that biking helps to ease the pain of arthritis, and helps to increase the effectiveness of their hands. The bicycle ergometer has been used for years in conjunction with cardiac research and rehabilitation projects because of the controlled stress that can be placed on the heart and vascular system.

Cycling has become a serious alternative to running as a popular fitness activity due to the many injury problems with running long distances over many years. Cycling eliminates the force and stress placed on the joints and the lower back that running causes. The rider does not have to support all of the body weight. In fact, the stationary bicycle (see Figure 1.4) is currently one of the most popular pieces of exercise equipment for home use on the market. It is being used in rehabilitative work as well as for normal cardiovascular maintenance. It can provide many attractive advantages such as these:

1. It can be used in inclement weather;
2. It is easier to use in the nondaylight hours;
3. It is safer for people to exercise within the home—especially for women and children;
4. It is easier to monitor the intensity and duration without the stop signs and traffic lights;
5. It is safer to ride than regular cycling because of traffic and various road hazards;
6. It is safer from an injury standpoint when compared to running because there is much less wear and tear on the knee joints and ligaments;
7. Insurance companies are more likely to recognize the stationary bike as a rehabilitary tool;
8. The rider can do other things during each ride, i.e., watch television, talk on the phone, or read a book.

As you can see, it is difficult to argue against the advantages of the stationary bicycle as a physical fitness tool. However, we believe that there are more benefits to cycling than just the physiological areas. If you are bicycling just for physiological benefits, you may want to consider just the stationary bicycle. However, you should understand that very few people are able to persist at cycling or any other physical activity when the only motivation is physical fitness. The stationary bicycle can get quite boring in a short period of time. For long-lasting results, it is best to learn to enjoy all of the benefits of cycling. We recommend that you consider all its benefits before purchasing a stationary bicycle. If you are bicycling for many reasons, you should consider regular cycling and possibly supplement it with a stationary bicycle. We recommend that you use both, but if you can only afford one, then buy a regular bicycle. Be sure to read the sections in Chapter 6 and Appendix A for the correct procedures on using the regular bicycle and the stationary bicycle for physical fitness.

Psychological Benefits

There is mounting evidence that regular physical activity such as running and cycling can have a positive impact on the mental outlook of people. There is a chemical basis to the positive feeling. Many believe that a brain hormone called beta endorphins is released during periods of vigorous activity. The hormone makes people feel good and experience a "natural high." William Glasser coined the term "positive addiction" and suggested that physical activity is an excellent way to improve the psychological state of people. Many psychologists and psychiatrists are actually prescribing various forms of physical activity for their patients with mental problems. This area is certainly not as well documented as the physiological area but there does seem to be much agreement that psychological benefits do occur for most active people.

Bicycle riders talk about the ability to unwind and relax during and after a vigorous ride. The feeling of the wind in your face and the enjoyment of the outdoor scenery is certainly a positive feeling that can improve one's mental outlook. Office workers mention the feeling of getting on a bicycle after a hard day at work and enjoying the solitude of a quiet ride home. Certainly, different people approach physical activity in many ways, but there does appear to be certain psychological benefits if the activity is approached with the right attitude.

Financial Benefits

Bicycling can be financially rewarding if you can substitute the bike for the automobile in certain situations. Riding to work, to the Post Office, to the store, and many other places (see Chapter 3 for lots of examples) can be done with a bicycle rather than a car. This can save on gas, oil, and upkeep on the car. In certain situations, the two car family can become a one car family if the bicycle can be used in place of a second car. This eliminates car insurance, gas, oil, and upkeep on the second car. By the same token, the three car family can become a two car family. The bicycle can also be a very convenient vehicle for dropping off the car when it needs repair. It can eliminate the need for someone else to drop you off and pick you up.

There is also evidence that active people are healthier and that they spend less money on health care and miss less work than people that are less active. This can be financially rewarding for many people depending on their type of occupation. It may also mean a better rate on life and medical insurance. Many insurance companies are offering special premiums for active, healthy people.

AN ENJOYABLE FORM OF PLAY

Play is a concept that is misunderstood by many people. Play as opposed to work is an activity that is enjoyed for no material or external reward. People engage in playful activities for the intrinsic, satisfying feelings. Play can take many different forms in different societies. In our society, common forms of play include activities focused on music, art, drama, sports, games, dance, and adventure. Specific examples include:

Figure 1.5   Cyclist loaded up for a camping excursion

Figure 1.6   Exploring on a mountain bike

1. Playing a round of golf on the weekend;
2. Acting in a community theater group;
3. Running in a 10-kilometer race;
4. Listening to a new record;
5. Taking a 10-mile bike ride into the country.

As you can see, these are many important self-satisfying activities that are common in our society. People will persist at these activities for a lifetime without any specific external gain. Of course, many of these activities do have additional benefits such as physiological improvements and financial savings, but it seems to be the play aspect that is the most motivating for many people. This is why we are encouraging you to take up cycling for the benefits of play rather than other reasons. The other benefits may occur and that is fine, but always try to use the bike for play and enjoyment first.

The bicycle is a great vehicle that many people use to enjoy the exploration of their local and surrounding areas. You will be surprised at how much more you can see from a bicycle than from a car. The bicycle can help you to find and enjoy many different areas in your vicinity. The use of the bicycle for exploring can also be extended into bicycle camping and touring (see Figure 1.5). More and more people are concerned about our vanishing wilderness and are seeking ways to explore and enjoy our environment. This might be a biking activity that will appeal to you. Refer to our section in Chapter 6 for more information on this use of the bike. This is the major reason that we are not totally in favor of the stationary bike because you cannot enjoy the outdoor scenery. We think that the exploration and enjoyment of the environment is an important reason for taking up cycling for life.

Some people have extended their use of the bicycle into racing activities. This can also be a fun and challenging form of play similar to the movement that has many runners participating in the various distance racing events. This may also be a form of play for you. It is possible to set some personal goals with regard to bicycle racing and it might be enjoyable to compete against yourself as you are getting started with your bicycle. Another advanced bicycling activity is the triathlon. The triathlon is an advanced competitive challenge that includes running, swimming, and bicycling. This also might appeal to you as another type of play. Refer to the section in Chapter 6 on advanced conditioning and training.

The various forms of play are an important part of what is referred to as the "good life." When people talk about the good life, we think of a long bicycle ride into the country on a nice sunny day or the adventure of exploring the desert or a new wooded trail on a mountain bike (see Figure 1.6). To us there are no better benefits to cycling than the aspects of play.

Buying a Bicycle

Probably the most important decision you will make when buying a bicycle is the type and quality of the bicycle. There are many types of bicycles available on the market today at many prices! First let's define and talk about the types of bicycles and then define the parts of a bicycle. You will need to know the language of bicycling and the types of bicycles before you can intelligently buy one. In a bicycle shop you will hear terms that you are not familiar with if you don't learn the bicycle language. We will take you through a bicycle part by part and teach you the language and terms used by bicyclists. Once you have learned to "talk bicycle" you will be more comfortable when you go to buy your bicycle. As you learn about bicycles and the parts of a bicycle you should visit several places that sell bicycles. Bicycle stores usually have better trained, more knowledgeable clerks (see our discussion later in the chapter).

There is no need to go out and buy a bicycle right away. You can learn all the skills you need with almost any bicycle. If you have an old clunker, use it to learn the skills. If you don't have a bicycle, rent or borrow one. Both authors of this book started with old used bicycles, and purchased their "good" bicycles later.

TYPES OF BICYCLES

As you probably have guessed from the previous discussion there are many types of bicycles on the market today. Let's investigate the different types of bicycles available for purchase.

In the 1960s there were only two basic adult bicycles one could buy: the 3-speed and the old standard balloon tire (coaster or paper delivery) bicycle. Then in the late 1960s the derailleur (10-speed) dropped handlebar bicycle became "the bicycle" to buy. The early 1970s saw the moto-cross bicycle (also called BMX) become popular with the young bicyclist. The adult cruiser (the old paper delivery bicycle with many modifications) became popular in the 1970s. The cruiser seems to be a spinoff from the moto-cross bicycle. As moto-cross riders got older they wanted the ride and feel of the moto-cross bicycle but did not want to ride the small moto-cross model. The newest bicycle on the market today is the all-terrain bicycle (also called the mountain bike). As you can see, the consumer today has to make a choice between several types of bicycles—3-speed, cruiser, mountain, derailleur, moto-cross. There is even a company that makes recumbent bicycles (bicycles that a person rides in a lying or sitting position).

The 3-Speed Bicycle

The 3-speed bicycle (also called the English racer) is a bicycle that can take lots of abuse. It has captured part of the bicycle market for years and will continue to do so. The 3-speed bicycle is less expensive to buy, takes less upkeep, and is more durable than the derailleur bicycle. The upright riding position is good for vision and you can shift gears when stopped. For short trips the 3-speed is excellent. For long trips and steep hills, it is not the bicycle of choice. The weight and limited gear selection make it an unacceptable touring and long-distance bicycle. It is also a slow bicycle; the name English racer is far from the truth since the bicycle is not a racing bicycle. There is nothing wrong with buying a 3-speed bicycle if you do not plan on touring, taking long rides, or climbing many hills (see Figure 2.1).

Investigate where you can rent or borrow bicycles. Inquire at the local police or government office as to the possibility of an auction of bicycles that have been found in the area.

Figure 2.1   3-speed bicycle

Figure 2.2   Adult cruiser

The Adult Cruiser

The adult cruiser is an excellent bicycle for riding around town and for short trips. Basically, it is an excellent alternative to the 3-speed bicycle. The cruiser has proven reliability and is usually an inexpensive bicycle to buy. If you want to spend more money you can fancy up the cruiser bicycle. Cruisers can come with 3-speed hubs or with derailleurs. If the cruiser has a 3-speed hub, it will come with coaster brakes in the back and caliper brakes in the front. The cruiser that has the rear derailleur has caliper brakes on both the front and rear wheels. What you have with the above equipment is an upright riding bicycle with balloon tires. The cruiser bicycle has all the options, except small light wheels, that you have with the 3-speed and derailleur bicycle. The weight of the cruiser is the biggest problem. It makes the cruiser a poor choice for long trips and for touring. The cruiser does give a really smooth ride and is easy to handle. It is also an excellent off-road bicycle. If you live around a lot of dirt roads the cruiser is an excellent choice for you (see Figure 2.2).

The Derailleur Bicycle

The derailleur (or 10-speed) bicycle with dropped handlebars is the most popular bicycle in the United States. The basic derailleur style is an excellent bicycle when used on paved roads for touring and for longer rides (over four miles). It is also a good short trip bicycle. It handles hills extremely well. The nemesis of the derailleur bicycle is the rough and unpaved road. A good derailleur bicycle will also require much more maintenance and care than the other bicycles already discussed. Price will vary, according to the type and quality of the components, from $70 for a department store special, to over $2000 for a custom made state-of-the-art bicycle. However, you can find good to excellent derailleur bicycles in the $150 to $400 range. Most mass market derailleur bicycles in this price range are excellent quality bicycles and offer a lot for the money. Competition from different manufacturers has kept the price down and even caused the price of good bicycles to drop in the last several years.

One of the authors of this book bought an excellent derailleur bicycle about eight years ago for approximately $350. When we did our research on prices of new bicycles, the same bicycle that cost about $350 then now cost $269! And the $269 bicycle is a better product than the older bicycle! The other author was able to buy a new derailleur bicycle for about $350 that was a couple of models up from the $269 model. As you can see, the price and quality of today's derailleurs make them a good buy. How often today do you see the price of a product go down and the quality go up? What you had to pay $300 for in the past now cost about $150 to $200. Of course you can have a derailleur custom-fitted and handcrafted for about $2000 to $3000 if you so desire. Yet, you would be hard-pressed to tell the difference between the custom-made bicycle and the good mass market bicycle (see Figure 2.3).

Figure 2.3   Derailleur bicycle

Figure 2.4   Recumbent bicycle

If you wish, you can even buy or make a derailleur recumbent bicycle. The recumbent is now on the mass market and costs about $500. The recumbents are very comfortable bicycles to ride but they are more difficult to steer than the regular derailleur. The recumbent derailleur bicycle makes better use of the leg muscles and therefore the rider can apply more power to the pedals than the nonrecumbent rider. The main problem with the recumbent bicycle is that it is difficult for cars to see the bicycle. Another problem with the recumbent is that it is not as easy to maneuver in traffic. Recumbents are great bicycles for the long trip but not for short trips. They are fun bicycles to own and to ride (see Figure 2.4).

The All-Terrain (Mountain) Bicycle

The all-terrain bicycle or mountain bicycle is a very strong and rugged bicycle that is a cross between the BMX (moto-cross), derailleur bicycle, and cruiser. The all-terrain bicycle is relatively lightweight and can handle the dirt road, but it has the gearing of the derailleur. The handlebars have been designed for strength, as have all the components of the all-terrain bicycle. The all-terrain bicycle is made for ruggedness and durability. However, they are not cheap bicycles; expect to pay over $500 for a good quality bicycle. The main weakness of the bicycle is that it is not good for long tours or extended riding. The all-terrain bicycle uses the large knobby tires and rims seen on cruisers. This is

Figure 2.5   All-terrain bicycle

Figure 2.6   Moto-cross bicycle

Visit several bicycle shops and see if you can identify the different types of bicycles discussed in this chapter. What bicycle did you most commonly see in the stores?

where a great part of the weight of the bicycle is found and this is what makes the all-terrain bicycle "off limits" to the serious touring enthusiast. However, some individuals do use all-terrain bicycles for touring (see Figure 2.5).

The BMX Bicycle

The BMX or moto-cross bicycle is a popular bicycle for younger people. It can be used for short course dirt track racing as well as pleasure riding. It is very durable but is not a good bicycle for riding back and forth to work. Our advice is to leave the BMX to the kids (see Figure 2.6).

PARTS OF A BICYCLE

The Frame

The main part of a bicycle is the frame. The frame consists of (1) a top tube, (2) a head tube, (3) a down tube, (4) a seat tube, (5) two seat stays, and (6) two chain stays (see Figure 2.7).

Bicycle frames also come in different sizes, from 19 inches to 27 inches. The different frame sizes are needed to fit different size bodies (a six footer needs a larger frame than a five footer). Bicycle frames are made of different size and quality tubes. The technology of tubing is always changing. Chrome-molybdenum, manganese, and vanadium alloy are currently the best "steels" for making bicycle tubing. Fiber-resin composites are also being used to make frames. When you buy your bicycle it would be best if you request up-to-date information concerning the "new steels" from your local bicycle shop. However, there are still only two types of tubing presently used in bicycle frame con-

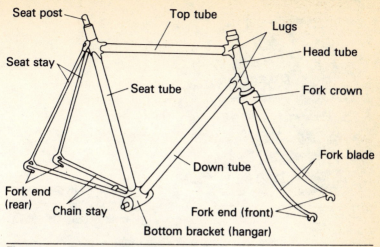

Figure 2.7 Frame with parts labeled

struction (straight gauge and double butted). The most common tubing used is the straight gauge; straight gauge tubing is not reinforced where it joins the other parts of the bicycle. Usually when straight gauge tubing is used, the joints are simple welds with no reinforcement (see Figure 2.8).

The second type of tube construction is the double-butted tube. Double-butted tubing is thicker at the ends where they are joined to the parts of the frame. Most frames that use double-butted tubing will also use lugs to join the tubes (see Figure 2.9)

The best bicycle frames are all made with double-butted tubing and complete lug construction for all parts of the frame. Some bicycle frames will only have the main tubes (seat, down, head, and top) made with double-butted tubing; the seat stays and chain stays are not double-butted. However, the very best and strongest frames will also have the seat and chain stays made of double-butted tubing. The fork should also be double-butted on the best bicycles. The best frames are also low temperature welded or brazed. High temperature welds and brazing can make the tubing brittle, and consequently it can develop fatigue breaks. Of course, a total double-butted lugged frame will cost much more than other frames. Only the hardcore cyclist will demand the best frames. For most individuals, a high tech frame is a waste of money. Most individuals simply do not need or appreciate such a frame. Our advice is to get a frame that is at least lugged, and if pos-

Figure 2.8 Simple weld on frame

Figure 2.9 Lugs on frame

sible, a frame with double-butted tubing in the main tubes. If you do not plan on really rough riding, you can get along with a frame that uses straight gauge tubing if it is chrome-molybdenum. At today's prices you can buy a chrome-molybdenum straight gauge tubing, lugged frame bicycle for about $150. Most department stores do not carry the more expensive bicycle frames.

A word of caution concerning buying used frames. Frames "get soft" (lose stiffness) and may not be a good buy even if they are high tech construction. Remember that most high tech frames are used by a real bicycle enthusiast and will have many miles on the frame (think of it as a used car with a lot of miles on the mileage gauge).

Frames are also available in several different shapes. The most common frame is the diamond-shaped model. Both men and women use this type because it is the strongest available. It represents 85–90 percent of the bicycle frame market. We recommend this type of frame.

The following is a checklist that can be used when buying a bicycle frame. The list is arranged from cheapest to most expensive for each category.

Type of Metal or Alloy Used
    plain steel   _____
    steel alloy   _____
    other materials   _____
Construction
    no lugs   _____
    partial lugs   _____
    all lugs   _____
Welding
    high temperature   _____
    low temperature   _____
Type of Tubing Used in Construction
    straight gauge   _____
    double-butted   _____
        main tubes   _____
        main and stays   _____
        all parts   _____

Many women prefer a "ladies" frame with the top tube in the dropped shape. These frames represent 10–15 percent of the market. They are not as strong as the diamond shape but should not be a problem under normal riding conditions around town. Some women prefer this style because of the historical tradition, the ease of mounting and riding wearing a dress or skirt, or the feeling that it is safer to ride. There are also frames for women called a "mixtie." These types have two parallel bars that run diagonally the length of the bicycle from the top of the headset to the attachment point for the rear wheel. The mixtie is stronger than the dropped-shape style.

    Don't feel uncomfortable about calling a bicycle shop. Most bicycle mechanics love to talk about frames and the most up-to-date ma-

Do this activity to get an idea of the prices of bicycles and frames. Call a bicycle shop and ask the prices for the following frames:

1. Steel frame, not lugged
2. Steel frame, lugged construction
3. Double-butted main tubes, lugged construction
4. Double-butted main tubes, chrome-molybdenum, lugged construction
5. All double-butted, chrome-molybdenum, lugged construction

terials used in bicycles. Also, don't be shocked by the price difference between frames. You can buy two complete inexpensive bicycles for the price of a good frame. Remember you get what you pay for in a bicycle frame.

The Brakes

There are two main types of brakes used on bicycles today: (1) caliper brakes and (2) coaster brakes. The caliper brake is activated by the hands using levers. The coaster brake is activated using the crank (pedals) in a reverse pedaling motion. The coaster brake only works on the rear wheel, while the caliper brake will work on front and rear wheels (see Figure 2.10).

Caliper brakes are made with either a center pull or side pull mechanism. There has been and will be arguments as to which type of caliper brake is the best. Both types of caliper brakes do an excellent job of stopping the bicycle if adjusted and maintained properly. There is a special type of caliper brake, called a cantilever (see Figure 2.11) that is found on many of the more expensive bicycles. The cantilever brake can apply more force to the rim and therefore stop the bike quicker. Many bicycles that are set up for touring have cantilever brakes. Mountain bicycles also have cantilever brakes.

Coaster brake

Caliper brake—
center pull

Caliper brake—
side pull

Figure 2.10   Brakes

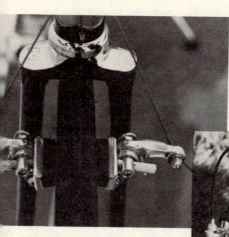

Figure 2.11   Cantilever brakes

Figure 2.12   Auxiliary brake lever

Some caliper brakes have an auxiliary lever (see Figure 2.12) sometimes called a suicide lever. The auxiliary lever will reduce the full movement of your primary lever, thus you lose braking power. We do not recommend the auxiliary lever.

The coaster brake is not as popular as the caliper brake. The reason for the lack of popularity is that the coaster brake cannot be used on derailleur bicycles (commonly known as 10-speed bicycles). This type of brake was used on all the old "one-speed" (Balloon tire) bicycles. The coaster brake has experienced a resurgence in popularity during the past few years because of the return of the balloon tire bicycle called the cruiser. Coaster brakes are excellent brakes but they just cannot be used on derailleur bicycles. When the derailleur bicycle captured the market in the 1970s the coaster brake became the "other" brake.

The Wheels

Wheels are always in the conversation when bicyclists get together and talk bicycles. Building a good wheel is one of the most difficult tasks for a bicycle mechanic. A wheel consists of a rim, spokes, hub, and tires (see Figure 2.13).

Hubs. Let's start from the inside of the wheel and progress to the outside. First there is the hub. There are several types of hubs one can buy (see Figure 2.14). For most bicycle riders a one-piece alloy hub with free-bearings is more than adequate. Some hubs have sealed bearings, and are difficult to repair. Most off-road bicycles will come with sealed hubs. Steel hubs are cheaper but have a tendency to break spokes. Aluminum hubs are more expensive, but there is less of a chance to break spokes. The most important thing to remember about hubs is that the bearings need to be greased unless you have sealed hubs, and therefore they must be able to be removed for servicing. See Chapter 5 for information about maintenance.

Spokes. Spokes come in heavy and lightweight gauges. They are made of steel or stainless steel. The spoke pattern is a matter of personal preference. Spoke patterns come in a one, two, and three-cross design. All patterns are adequate for most bicyclists. If you plan on track racing, you may want a different pattern. The three-cross design is the most common and is the pattern preferred by most bicycle riders. As long as the spokes are tightly laced you will have very few problems with

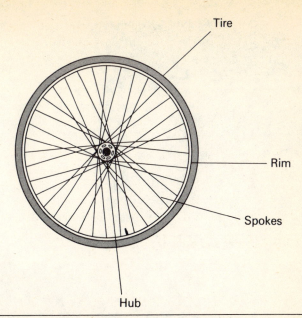

Figure 2.13 Wheel with hub, spokes, tire, and rim

any of the spoke patterns. We prefer the stainless steel three-cross pattern spoked wheel (see Figure 2.15). The stainless steel spoke lasts longer and is a stronger spoke. If your body weight is over 190 pounds you may want to invest in heavy gauge stainless steel spokes (or double-butted spokes). The investment in these spokes will pay off with fewer broken spokes, fewer bent rims, and fewer headaches!

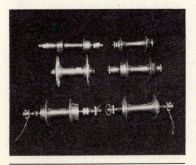

Figure 2.14 Hubs

Figure 2.15 Three-cross spoke pattern

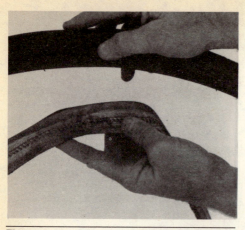

Figure 2.16   Clincher and tubular tires

Figure 2.17   Clincher and tubular rims

Rims and Tires.   Rims depend on your choice of tires. There are two types of tires: clincher and tubular (see Figure 2.16).

The tubular tire, also called a sew-up, is very expensive ($30–$40 per tire), and does not last very long. However, the tubular tire is also very light, and rolls with less friction than the clincher tire. Weight is the biggest problem with bicycles; especially weight that is in the wheels. The real hard-core bicyclist will buy, and keep on buying, tubulars to save the weight. The tubular tire is mounted to the rim with glue and is a messy job. The bicyclists who use tubulars pay more than just money to use them; sometimes they go mad replacing the tires. As you might be able to tell, we do not recommend the use of tubular tires

Go to a bicycle shop or any other place that will have a lot of bicycles. See if you can tell the clincher and tubular rim and tire apart. See if you can find different types of brakes and spoke patterns.

for the general bicyclist. We do not feel the tubular tire is a good choice of tires for anyone but the bicycle racer. Special rims are also needed for the tubular tire. You cannot use the same rim for tubulars and clincher tires.

The clincher tire (heavier but much less expensive than the tubular) is much like the automobile tire. The tire is held on by a bead that locks under the edge of the rim. Rims for the clincher tire come in several designs and weights. As might be expected, the rim can be made of steel or steel alloys, and rims come in different widths (wide and narrow). The width is of little importance since tires are available for both widths. Try to buy a rim that is made of aluminum or a steel alloy since it will resist bending better than the steel rim (see Figure 2.17).

Handlebars, Stems, and Headset

Handlebars. Handlebars come in raised or dropped styles. The type of handlebar you buy will dictate your riding position (see Figure 2.18 for handlebar types).

Handlebars are made of either steel or aluminum alloy. Aluminum is the best choice of material unless you plan on track racing. The raised handlebar comes in several styles. The traditional raised handlebar is seen on 3-speed bicycles (called the north road bend handlebar). There are other styles of raised handlebars that are seen on dirt bicycles and off-road bicycles. If you think you would like a raised or upright handlebar, try several styles and choose one that fits your comfort level. By the way, there is no reason why an upright or raised handlebar cannot be used with the derailleur bicycle. Many people prefer the upright position when riding a bicycle but want the performance of the derailleur bicycle. The solution is simple: have the bicycle shop

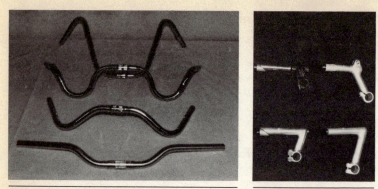

| Figure 2.18   Handlebar types | Figure 2.19   Stems |

swap handlebars (swap the dropped style for the north road bend handlebar). *Do not* be pressured into a dropped style handlebar only because most derailleur bicycles use that style.

There are two general patterns for dropped handlebars: the maes bend and randonneur bend. Either type is adequate for the general bicyclist. The randonneur is used more for touring bicycles, but can be used by the nontouring bicyclist (see Figure 2.18).

Stems.   Stems come in different sizes and are made with different types of steel. The stem is used to connect the handlebars to the bicycle at the head tube. Different stem lengths are needed to fit bicycles to different size bodies. More about fitting the bicycle will be discussed later in this chapter. Most good stems are made of steel alloy or aluminum. If you adjust your stem upward be sure that it is not raised past the safety mark on the stem. It could fall out and cause an accident. When setting up your bicycle the seat and stem should be about the same level. Otherwise you will be leaning forward or backward too much. If you plan on racing your bicycle, you will want to have the seat higher than the stem (see Figure 2.19).

Headset.   The headset is found inside the head tube and usually consists of two sets of bearings. The bearings are held in place by cones and cups. The reason for the headsets is to allow the fork to turn inside the head tube. Good bicycles come with good headsets while cheap bicycles come with cheap headsets. Proper adjustment of the headset will keep the bearings from wearing too quickly (see Chapter 5 for information about maintenance of the headset).

Cranks, Bottom Brackets, and Pedals

Crank Set.   Cranks (the big wheel that the chain goes around) come in steel and alloys. The parts of a crank set are the chainring, crank arm, and axle. All good bicycles have alloy cranks. Steel cranks can still be found, but they only will be found on inexpensive bicycles. The better cranks are "cotterless." Cotterless cranks use bolts or nuts to attach the crank arm to the axle. Crank arms that attach to the axle by pins are called cottered cranks (see Figure 2.20). Our advice is to stay away from steel cottered cranks. The cottered crank tends to loosen up and wear very quickly, and they are difficult to remove and maintain.

Cotterless crank

Cottered crank

Figure 2.20   Cranks

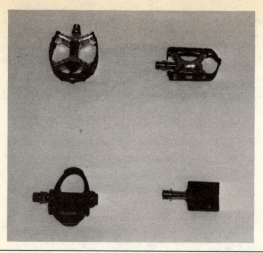

Figure 2.21   Pedals

Bottom Bracket.   The place where the crank fits into the frame is called the bottom bracket. Two sets of bearings (one on each side of the bottom bracket) support the crank axle. Good bearings are a must here. The bearings should be set into a removable retainer to aid in maintenance of the crank; this is not necessary if you have sealed bearings.

Pedals and Toe Clips.   Pedals come in several styles and several price ranges. The cheapest pedal is the rubber tread pedal without removable bearings. Most good bicycles come with metal pedals, that have bearings at each end. Steel pedals are almost indestructible. The lightweight alloy pedals (except titanium) will not take as much punishment as the steel pedal. A good set of steel pedals will be a wise investment. Pedals often come with toe clips.

Toe clips keep the feet in the proper pedaling position, but are somewhat difficult to get your feet into properly. Many people swear by them while others avoid them. They allow you to use the muscles on the back of the leg as well as the muscles on the front of the leg when pedaling the bicycle. If you are doing a lot of riding where you need to remove your foot from the pedal at stoplights or stop signs, you may wish to buy half-clips (see Figure 2.21). Some bicyclists use the regular toe clip without the straps for town riding. Try toe clips before you make up your mind. Chapter 3 has several learning activities for using toe clips.

Derailleurs

Derailleurs are the devices that move the chain from cog to cog on the freewheel (rear gears) and from chainring to chainring on the crank set. In other words, the derailleur is a gear-changing device. It changes the gears by lifting or pushing the chain. There are different types of derailleurs for the rear freewheel and the front crank. Today's derailleurs are excellent pieces of equipment. Even the low-cost derailleur with proper adjustment and proper maintenance is very reliable. Derailleurs are made of all types of material and come in many price ranges. We have used several brands and have found all major brands of derailleurs to be satisfactory. Stay in the $10 to $25 range for derailleurs. Below $10 you can get junk and above $25 you are paying for a high tech derailleur that you probably do not need (see Figure 2.22).

rear

front

Figure 2.22 Derailleur

Saddles (Seats)

The best saddles used to be made of leather and took a long time to break in. New saddles with modern designs do not need to be broken in. The selection of a saddle is very important for comfort. A poor fitting saddle will cause irritation, blisters, and general chafing. Invest in a good saddle that fits. Sit on all the saddle styles. Do not buy any saddle that does not feel comfortable right away! A bicycle saddle is like running shoes, if it does not fit well and feel good, do not buy it, no matter how good the bargain. We prefer the Avocet model saddle. Avocet has several different models for both men and women. Many bicycle shops will permit you to try the saddle on a long ride.

Freewheel and Chains

Freewheel. The freewheel, also known as a cluster, is the group of cogs that screw onto the rear hub. It is called a freewheel because it allows the rear wheel to coast when the rider is not pedaling. The selection of the cogs on the freewheel is how you control your gearing. Larger cogs (more teeth) produce lower (easier) gearing, smaller cogs (fewer teeth) produce higher (harder) gearing. If you will be climbing a lot of hills, you will want a freewheel that has lower gears. If you will be riding your bicycle on flat land, you will want a freewheel with higher gears. Most freewheels that you will see are intermediately geared; that is to say, they do not have a very low or a very high gear. The freewheel wheel section comes with five or six cogs. The better freewheels have cogs that can be replaced individually. The less expensive freewheels come as one piece so you cannot replace only one cog. If you wear out one cog on a solid freewheel you must replace the complete freewheel. This is not as bad as it sounds since the less expensive freewheels are good products. It is best to buy a freewheel that is made of steel since it lasts a lot longer and is a *lot* cheaper. You can replace a freewheel for about $15 (see Figure 2.23). See Appendix B for a gearing chart to use when replacing freewheels for racing or touring.

Chains. Chains are the means for transmitting power to the rear wheel. It is best to stay with a good chain. Chains will stretch and wear out. A good chain will last about 1500 to 2000 miles. Quality chains cost about $8 to $10. We have found that if you pay more than the above price you do not get that much more for the money and they do not last

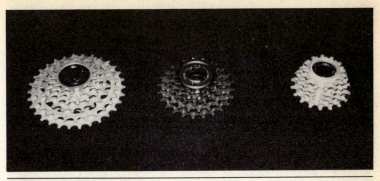

Figure 2.23   Freewheels

longer. There is a significant difference between the cheap chain and the more expensive chain. You will pay about twice as much ($4 versus $8) for the more expensive chain but you will get about five times longer chain life.

FITTING THE BICYCLE FRAME

Now that you have some information concerning the types of bicycles and parts on the market, let's move to fitting a bicycle frame to your body. The fit of the frame is important for comfort and proper riding mechanics. Many of the bicycles discussed in the previous section come in different frame sizes. Frame size normally varies from 19 inches to 27 inches. The larger the body the bigger the frame size.

There are two good ways for you to check proper frame size. The first and best way to check your frame size is to stand over the bicycle (straddle the top tube) with both feet flat on the ground. Do not wear shoes for this test. The top tube should be about 1/2- to 1-inch below your crotch. If the distance is more than 1-inch, do not buy the bicycle. If you cannot put your feet on the ground, do not buy the bicycle. Many bicyclists fit the frame right up to the crotch. The second method of determining frame size is to add 10 inches to your leg length. This method is only used to get an estimate concerning frame size. A typical six-foot person will take a frame size of 24 to 25 inches. The other important fit for your bicycle frame is the saddle to handlebar length (see Figure 2.24).

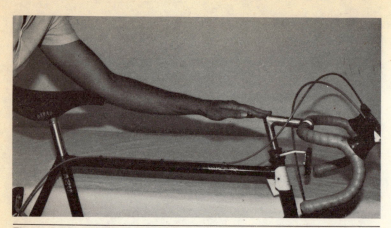

Figure 2.24   Saddle to stem fit

The distance from the handlebar to the tip of the saddle should be about the length of your fingers and forearm. Place your elbow against the saddle and extend your arm toward the handlebars. Your fingers should be within 1/2-inch of touching the handlebar. If your fingers are 1/2-inch over or 1/2-inch under the correct distance the fit is excellent. If a change in stem length will adjust the distance within the 1/2-inch criterion, then the frame fits. About three inches can be corrected for in stem length. We are assuming that your fingers come to at least the bolt of the stem. If your fingers do not come to the bolt of the stem, the top tube of the frame is too long.

There are several "fit kits" that many bicycle stores use or have in stock (i.e., Bill Farrell Fit Kit, Bill Boston Accufit). These kits are very good and you may want to investigate the use of such a kit to fit a bicycle. Most individuals who use the fit kits are very serious bicyclists such as racers.

Take your present bicycle and determine if the frame is the proper size. Also, go to a bicycle store and try several bicycles for proper fit. Investigate the use of a "fit kit."

Find a good place to buy bicycles. Ask other people who own bicycles where they bought their bicycles. Call bicycle clubs and ask for their advice on good shops. If you live in a town with a college or university call the bike co-op and ask for information concerning good bicycle shops. Most people are willing to supply answers to your questions about good bicycle shops. You can bet you will find where *not* to buy your bicycle.

WHERE TO BUY YOUR BICYCLE

Our advice is for you to deal with a reputable bicycle shop. Discount stores, warehouse department stores, etc., usually do not have trained clerks to help fit a bicycle. As a matter of fact, most such stores only carry two size frames (19 and 23 inch). Look around and ask questions before you choose a shop. Look at the type of bicycle sold in the store. Look at the selection of bicycles they have in stock. If you want a 3-speed, be sure they stock several brands of 3-speeds. Some bicycle shops will only stock certain types of bicycles.

Service after sale is important. Check with the Better Business Bureau to see if the store has unsettled complaints. All new bicycles will need some adjustment. Ask about adjustment periods. Good shops will ask you to bring the bicycle back after about 200 miles for a tune-up (without charge as part of the service). Ask about test rides. If the shop will not allow test rides do not buy there. Check the bicycle on the test ride for any problems. Check the balance (see if you can ride it with no hands). Be sure the bicycle does not pull to one side. Check the brakes and make sure all the equipment works.

Before you buy the bicycle ask about warranties. *Get the warranties in writing.* If you find a bicycle you like and if it fits well, but if the components are not what you want, ask about changing the components (i.e., raised handlebars for dropped). Remember it costs the bicycle shop money in labor to change components; therefore be reasonable about the added cost if you have components changed. Do not expect the shop to make several changes without charge. Most shops will make one or two simple component changes at no additional charge.

ADJUSTING YOUR BICYCLE

If you buy your bicycle from a good bicycle shop, the adjustments will be made by the clerk or mechanic on duty when you pick up your bicycle. If you have an old bicycle and you wish to make the adjustments yourself, they are not hard to do. You should learn how to make these adjustments. We call it fine-tuning your bicycle. When all the adjustments are made, you should be comfortable on the bicycle, and you will be in the most advantageous position to apply power to the pedals.

Saddle height is the first and most important adjustment you will need to make. Adjustment of the saddle will determine the efficiency of the cyclist. Two basic saddle adjustments can be made as follows: (1) saddle height and (2) saddle tilt. The saddle height is the most important of the two adjustments. Scientific studies have shown that this adjustment can affect power output by 5–10 percent. The most acceptable and most common way to adjust the saddle height is to make the height 109 percent of the inseam leg measurement. To adjust the saddle height do the following procedure:

1. Measure the inseam length of your leg (the bottom of your foot to your crotch).
2. Multiply the above length by 109 percent.
3. Place the crank arm parallel to the seat tube so that the pedal is at the bottom of its swing (see Figure 2.25).
4. Now make the distance from the pedal to the top of the saddle the 109 percent measure (see Figure 2.25).

A word of advice: Many people feel uncomfortable with this length at first, but it will become very comfortable in a short time. If you lower the saddle, your efficiency will decrease and you will work harder riding your bicycle.

The tilt of the saddle is for comfort only. Most good bicyclists have the nose of the saddle higher than the back. But this is a matter of choice, and does not increase or decrease the efficiency of the bicyclist. Only good saddles have adjustments for tilt. Experiment with saddle tilt and find your comfort zone.

Make the adjustments we have talked about on your bicycle. Adjust saddle height, saddle tilt, brake levers, and toe clips.

After the saddle height and tilt have been set, the next adjustment is the saddle to handlebar length. We talked about this measurement in the previous section on fitting the frame. The saddle can be moved forward a little, but the major adjustment is made by replacing the stem with a different length stem. After making the saddle to handlebar length adjustment, make sure the top of the stem is the same height as the saddle.

You can also adjust (move) the brake levers on the handlebars. Move them to where they are easy to reach and comfortable for you. The major objective in moving the brake levers is to have them where you can get to them. If you have to move too far to reach the brake levers it could be a safety problem.

If you have toe clips, they should be adjusted for the type of riding you are doing. If you are riding in traffic and will need to stop often,

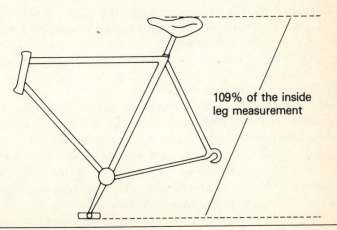

109% of the inside leg measurement

Figure 2.25   Saddle adjustment

adjust the strap so that you can get your foot out of the clip with ease. If you are on a long extended trip with few stops, tighten the straps up so that the foot and pedal make firm contact. Also be sure to buy the proper size toe clip. Toe clips come in different size lengths (small, medium, large). Buy the length that puts the ball of the foot over the axle of the pedal.

OTHER EQUIPMENT

When buying a bicycle you should also consider buying other equipment that will make your bicycle riding more enjoyable and safe.

The most common item that people buy is some type of device for carrying things, such as books, groceries, etc. If you are going to ride your bicycle for other than just pure pleasure you should invest in some sort of carrier for your bicycle. Many students use backpacks for carrying books when riding their bicycles. The backpack is a good way to carry items, but it also places extra weight on your back. It would be better to let the bicycle carry the weight. This means using some type of device that is hooked to the bicycle. There are a wide variety of baskets and panniers (panniers are the cloth bags that attach to the frame) that you can buy at bicycle shops (see Figure 2.26).

Panniers are used by bicyclists that tour because they are somewhat weatherproof and have several pockets in which to store items. Panniers are also easy to remove and could be considered as small suitcases that attach to the frame of a bicycle. If you plan on doing any touring, panniers are the best choice of carriers. However, it is hard to fit a large grocery bag into a pannier. So if you will be carrying large items on your bicycle, you may wish to invest in a large basket. Also remember that panniers are easy to steal and you may have to remove them whenever you stop and go into stores.

Most baskets are put on the rear of the bicycle. We feel that the rear basket is safer than a front basket. A basket that goes on the front attaches to the handlebars and makes steering difficult when heavy objects are placed in it. Baskets for the rear come in several sizes. There is also a rear basket that folds up when not in use. Child carriers are also placed on the rear of the bicycle. The child carrier can also be used to carry other items when not transporting a child.

Another type of carrier that you may wish to buy is a bicycle carrier for your car. There are several brands of carriers on the market, and

Baskets

Panniers

Figure 2.26   Equipment

they all do an adequate job of carrying bicycles. There are two basic types of bicycle carriers: (1) rooftop and (2) rear carrier. Depending on your car either type will do the job well. One word of warning: If you use a rooftop carrier be sure that your car and bicycle will make it under your garage door and other low underpasses. If you own a van this could be a major problem. The bicycle and van could come to a total height of over 11 or 12 feet.

Safety equipment will be discussed in Chapter 4. We consider lights, helmets, and reflectors as safety equipment and they are covered in Chapter 4. The choice of a helmet is important. Several brands and types of helmets are on the market today. Some helmets have better ventilation than other helmets. Ventilation is extremely important if you live in a hot climate. Try several helmets; they all feel different but buy the one that is comfortable.

If you live in an area that has lots of thorns that puncture tires, you should consider buying thorn resistant tubes for your bicycle. The name is a little misleading; your tires will still pick up thorns but you will not get as many flats. You can also buy a special plastic insert that goes inside the tire. If you buy both the thorn resistant tube and the plastic insert, you will find that flat tires from thorns will be a rare occurrence. However, you must remember that the added weight of the heavy tube and insert will affect your tire and rim weight. The weight of the wheel and rim is what most serious bicyclists try to keep to a minimum. Lower wheel weights usually lead to better bicycle performance. Both authors use thorn resistant tubes and feel the "drop" in performance is well worth the decrease in the number of flat tires. See Chap-

Look at different bicycles and see the type of baskets or carriers you see on them. Check with stores and find out prices of different types of baskets and carriers.

ter 5 for more information concerning the installing of the plastic protectors.

You may wish to buy bicycle gloves. Bicycle gloves are fingerless and usually are padded in the palms. The gloves help prevent ulnar nerve problems and protect the hands if you fall. The ulnar nerve problem comes from the pressure of the handlebars on your palm. Your hands will go numb after a long ride without gloves, because the ulnar nerve is being compressed. If you plan on riding for more than half an hour at a time on a derailleur dropped handlebar bicycle, buy gloves.

Along with gloves you may want to add handlebar grips to your handlebars. The modern handlebar grip is made of a lightweight material that absorbs road shock. They also cut down on ulnar nerve problems and will be well worth the cost. Many bicycles come with grips already on the bicycle from the factory. They come in many colors to match the color of your bicycle. Again, if you plan to take any long trips with your bicycle we recommend that you buy handlebar grips (see Figure 2.27).

A water bottle and a pump can be worth the investment. When you have a flat tire and are miles and miles from a repair shop, the pump is well worth the cost! Along with the pump you should buy a small repair kit that you can use on the road. The kit should include small tire irons to help remove the tire. Pumps and water bottles are attached to the frame of the bicycle and are easy to steal, so be sure to take them with you when you leave the bicycle. See Chapter 5 for more details about tools and tool kits.

Locks are a sad, but a necessary part, of modern life. Good bicycles invite stealing if not properly locked with a good *strong* lock. Given enough time any lock can be cut or broken. Therefore, when buying your lock be sure it is a lock that is difficult to cut or break. Two basic locking systems are used on most bicycles. One is the U-bar type lock

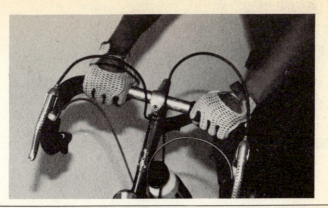

Figure 2.27   Gloves and handlebar grips

and system and the other is the cable or chain locking system (see Figure 2.28).

Remember to lock both wheels and the frame. Also remember to lock the bicycle to a post. Otherwise thieves will pick up the bicycle and carry it off to work on the lock later. If you use the U-bar lock you will have to take off your front wheel and lock it to the back wheel and frame. Always lock your bicycle in an area that is in full view of people. Bicycle thieves do not like to work where there is a lot of people traffic. A bicycle locked in an area of little traffic gives the thief time to break the lock.

Figure 2.28   Locking systems and locks

Buying a Bicycle

If you have a U-bar lock, practice removing the front wheel and locking your bicycle with the front wheel locked to the back wheel and frame.

, Quick release mechanisms are available for brakes, hubs, and saddles. Quick release wheels can be removed without tools. Quick release hubs are a must if you use a U-bar locking system. They are also handy when you have a flat on the road. If you get quick release hubs be sure to get quick release brakes. The quick release mechanism on the brake opens up the caliper brake to allow the rim and tire to pass through without undue force. If you buy quick release hubs be sure to

Hubs

Brakes

Saddles

Figure 2.29   Quick release mechanisms

Figure 2.30 Cuff clips

check them each time you ride. We have seen bicycle riders lose their front wheel at stoplights. The quick release mechanism usually does not come loose on its own. However, people have been known to fool around with bicycles that are locked and unattended (see Figure 2.29).

There is a complete line of special clothing for bicycling: shorts, shirts, shoes, hats, etc. For those that are concerned about clothing you can find several types and brands of excellent bicycling clothes. If you buy toe clips you may wish to buy special bicycle shoes. The bicycle shoe has cleats on the bottom to grip the pedal.

If you plan on riding your bicycle wearing long pants, then you should buy cuff clips. These clips come in cloth or steel. The cloth type uses a velcro fastener and takes more time to put on than the steel clip. You could use a rubber band if you wish; they are just a little harder to put on the cuffs. The whole idea of the clip is to keep your cuff away from the chain. By keeping the cuff off the chain it keeps the pants clean, and more importantly, out of the moving parts of the bicycle (see Figure 2.30).

If you live in an area that has lots of rain you might want to buy fenders for your bicycle. Fenders keep the rear wheel from throwing dirty water on your back. Fenders also keep the caliper brake from caking up with mud. You can even buy fenders that are detachable.

Many new bicycles (especially the derailleur style) do not come with a kickstand. You may want to invest in a good lightweight kickstand. If you do not have a kickstand, you will always need to lean the bicycle against a wall, or find a bicycle rack. At times walls and racks are hard to find.

Use the following checklist as a guide for buying a new bicycle. Determine the type of bicycle and the equipment you wish on the bicycle.

1. Frame
   _____ all steel construction, no lugs
   _____ steel construction, lugged
   _____ steel alloy not double butted, lugged
   _____ steel alloy double butted, lugged
       _____ double-butted only main tubes
       _____ double-butted total bicycle

2. Derailleur System
   _____ set up with low gears (hill climbing)
   _____ set up with intermediate gears
   _____ set up with high gears (flat land and racing)

3. Crank
   _____ cotterless
   _____ cottered

4. Handlebars
   _____ dropped
   _____ upright

5. Saddle
   _____ touring
   _____ standard

6. Tires, Rims, Hubs
   _____ steel rims
   _____ lightweight alloy rims
   _____ clincher tires
   _____ tubular (sew-ups) tires
   _____ quick release hubs (sealed or open)

7. Accessories
   _____ lights
   _____ helmet
   _____ pump
   _____ toe clips
   _____ cuff clips
   _____ lock

_____ clothing
_____ baskets, panniers
_____ bicycle carrier
_____ kickstand
_____ gloves
_____ handlebar grips
_____ water bottle
_____ tool kit
_____ bicycle shoes

UPGRADING EQUIPMENT

After you have used your bicycle for a period of time you may wish to upgrade some equipment. Most of the time upgrading means buying lighter and more expensive equipment. If you have a good frame that you are happy with you can then upgrade any component with better equipment. If you are not happy with your frame, it is best to buy a new bicycle.

Most individuals upgrade their wheels first. The total weight of a bicycle is important, but the weight of the wheels is the most important single component of the total weight. Too much weight in the wheels means you will work very hard at moving the bicycle. Most bicyclists will go to a tubular tire (remember tubulars take a different rim than clinchers). The tubular tire reduces the wheel weight dramatically. Wheel weight can be reduced if you are using a steel rim by buying a lighter weight rim. Try lighter weight rims before buying tubulars. Many bicycle shops will let you try new rims before buying.

After upgrading the wheels the next most common upgrade is the derailleur system. Most bicyclists will go from a 5-cog to a 6-cog freewheel. Many times the rear derailleur is also changed. However, be sure to talk with a good bicycle mechanic before making changes in the derailleur and the derailleur system. All components must fit and work together. Our basic advice on upgrading is to talk with several knowledgeable people before making any changes.

You will find a comprehensive checklist to use when buying a bicycle in the Sport Experience (see p. 46).

Incorporating Cycling into Your Lifestyle

After making decisions about becoming a cyclist (Chapter 1), and purchasing a bicycle and the necessary equipment (Chapter 2), you should begin to use your bicycle in many ways. There are many cycling activities that will help you to become more comfortable with your bicycle. There are also many motivational strategies that can help you to become a regular bicycle rider. It is important that the beginning rider realize that cycling can easily become part of a person's lifestyle. A slow, gradual process should be used with all activities. Remember that you have all the time you need to become proficient at learning to enjoy your bicycle. Too many beginners in any activity tend to overdo the activity and become sore, frustrated, and discouraged. This can lead to a quick burnout and a loss of interest in the activity. Bicycling should be thought of as an enjoyable lifelong activity. There is no hurry to learn skills and condition yourself—take your time and enjoy the process.

Your age, physical condition, and bicycling experience will be important factors as to how fast you can proceed with the use of the bike. Do not become discouraged with your lack of speed in progressing in these bicycling activities. Anyone can learn the necessary skills to enjoy bicycling, it just takes a little time and practice. It is not important to embark on an extensive preconditioning program for bicycling. The best way to get yourself ready to enjoy bicycling is to start biking slowly and to be sure that you do not overdo any activity. It is better to start slow than to start fast and hurt yourself, or become so sore that you can hardly walk and perform your daily activities. If you have not been riding a bicycle on a regular basis, initially, you will probably experience some muscle soreness in the hands, arms, legs, lower back, and backside. This is all quite normal and should not worry you unless the pain is extreme. Extreme muscular pain means that you probably have overdone the activity and you should slow down and reduce your distances. Stretching after a ride may help to reduce some of the delayed soreness. You have to remember that all the beginning soreness will slowly disappear as you condition your body with these cycling activities. Remember the slow, gradual process that we recommended for beginners.

Incorporating cycling into your lifestyle will require that you develop and maintain a certain fitness level and a certain skill level for handling your bike. If you develop these two areas, bicycling should become a positive, enjoyable activity that you can use in many ways for many years. This chapter will provide many activities that are aimed at developing both of these important aspects in bicycling success. No matter what your current fitness level or bicycling skill level, the completion of the activities in this chapter will help you to reach a level of proficiency with the bike so that you will want to continue using your bike for the rest of your life.

GETTING STARTED—PLACES TO BICYCLE

Since you already own a bike and accessories, you have no doubt already started thinking about how you can use your bike and the places where you can ride. With the addition of various racks, carriers, and panniers, the bike can be ridden to many places and used for many activities that a beginning cyclist probably has not considered. We would like to expand your thinking on how bicycling can be incorporated into your lifestyle.

There are many good possibilities to consider as places to begin riding your bike. The distance involved, the traffic conditions, the weather conditions, and your skill level will all be important to consider before you decide if each is a possibility for you and your situation. Remember that you may want to set some gradual goals with regard to riding to these places. For example, you may want to ride your bike only half the way to where you work because of the distance. A bicycle carrier on your car will enable you to park about halfway to work and ride the rest of the distance. We will make some suggestions within the discussion of each place to ride.

One of the first activities that we suggest is for you to sit down and write a list of all of the possible uses of your bike and the specific places where you can ride the bike. You may want to classify these places into three categories of short, medium and long rides. Of course, these categories will be different for every individual because of the fitness and skill level of the person. A short ride for one person could be a long ride for another person, but there is no need to worry about what anyone else thinks about your bicycling skill level.

Riding to Work or School

An excellent way of incorporating bicycling into your lifestyle is to ride to work or school every day or at least several days each week. It can become a good habit that offers many advantages for the cyclist. Many companies provide shower and changing facilities for recreational activities before and after working hours. These can be used for changing to and from bicycling gear. A nearby health club or spa could also be used for changing clothes. If the distance is not too great and the weather conditions are not too extreme, a change of clothes may not be necessary. The problem of clothes can be solved in several ways. Clothes can be folded and carried in bicycle panniers or they can be left ahead of time in a locker. Many types of raingear are available for inclement weather conditions.

A bicycle carrier for your car or truck can be used to help you start the process of becoming comfortable with riding to work. You can drive the car and park it varying distances from work in order to slowly increase the bicycling distance. There are probably many public places to park along your route to work. A shopping center or a public road are good examples of places to park and lock your bike. Sometimes your employer will provide bicycle racks near the automobile parking lots. Other times a post or pole of some type will be available. In some cases, an indoor closet or storage area can also be used. Bicycling to work or school can generate problems but every problem has many solutions and we think that the advantages outweigh the disadvantages in this situation.

Riding Around Town

Here are several suggestions for places you can bicycle to close to home:

Most of us live within a relatively short distance of a Post Office. It can be one of the definite bicycle trips that can be added to your growing list of bicycle rides. Panniers or a small backpack can usually hold the materials that need to be carried to the Post Office.

A neighborhood drugstore or hardware store is usually another regular stop for most of us and often is not too far away. Many small items can be carried without great difficulty. Be careful with large items that may be a problem to carry while maintaining control of the bicycle.

You can use your bicycle to do a certain portion of the grocery shopping depending upon the number of people that must be fed. A carrier can be pulled if large amounts of food need to be purchased (see Figure 3.1). Small bags of food can be carried in panniers and a backpack. A good habit is to use the bicycle for any extra trips to the store for small items such as milk, bread, or extra items that were forgotten during the regular trip. Avoid buying glass containers if at all possible.

A fun idea is to regularly ride your bike out to eat once a week or so. Get up early and take a breakfast ride or meet someone for lunch. There are numerous possibilities for using the bicycle in this manner.

Figure 3.1   Bike carrier for groceries

Pick out and obtain the directions to a city park, museum, zoo, library, community bicycle path, or any other point of interest. Visit this point of interest on your bicycle.

You have to be careful about evening meals because you may end up riding home in the dark (see Chapter 4 for safety tips for riding in the dark).

Exploring Nearby

The bicycle is excellent for exploring nearby areas because you can see much more from a bike than from a car. Start out in a different direction each day that you can use your bike for exploring.

Riding to a Picnic, Hiking, or Camping Area.   There may be areas within your location that can be reached by bicycle for a picnic or short hike. These could last a half day, full day, or even be an overnight trip (see Chapter 6 for details on overnight trips). A lunch could be packed or purchased at the site. It is a good way to explore and get to know the surrounding area. Be sure to remember the progression concept discussed earlier because you do not want to take a trip that is too long and too difficult for your capabilities. It is best to start nice and easy. If the specific area is too far away, you may want to use your bicycle carrier on the car to carry the bikes for a portion of the distance. This concept can be used for any of the trips that you plan with your bike. We do not think that it is necessary to impress anyone with how far or fast you are going on your bike.

Riding to Public Events.   There are many public events such as athletic contests, parades, concerts, movies, etc., where lots of people and cars will be present. Riding a bicycle can be an enjoyable change of pace from the madness of driving, parking, and scrambling in and out of a public event. Many times you can even beat the traffic, save a few dollars on parking, and get a little exercise. However, it is important to get off the main roads as soon as possible to avoid the rush of the traffic.

Riding to an Appointment. All of us have regular appointments with the eye doctor, the dentist, the beautician, the barber, etc. Many of these could be put on the list of places where the bicycle could be used instead of the car. Often, these places are in your immediate neighborhood. Many times it is simply a matter of scheduling a little extra time for the use of the bicycle.

Riding the Bike for Errands. There are many nearby errands such as taking the car to a garage for maintenance, borrowing equipment from a neighbor, going to the public library, withdrawing money from the bank, dropping off a roll of film to be developed, or trading paperback books with a relative that can be taken care of by using a bicycle. It is a good habit to use the bicycle to take care of many of these errands.

Taking an Exercise/Pleasure Ride. A bicycle ride can be planned for a morning or evening as part of a regular exercise/pleasure program. These rides can be to a specific place or they could be for a specific amount of time.

Some people enjoy these rides in the morning before work while others prefer riding after work in the evening. Experiment with both and find out what is best for you. We think that using the bike for exercise is best maintained when individuals can find a way to enjoy the activity process. We suggest that you concentrate on the scenery, your improvement in physical condition, or ride with a friend and enjoy the social interaction. Different people enjoy different aspects of the activity process.

Take a fitness ride. A resting heart rate check could be taken at the beginning of the ride and then another heart rate check during the ride and finally another heart rate check at the end of the ride. With a little experience, you can attempt to reach a target heart rate (see Chapter 6) during certain fitness rides.

Riding with the Family

Almost all of the aforementioned bicycle rides can be done with your family and friends. This appeals to many people as a positive feature of bicycling. It is also a good idea for parents to start children riding their bikes to various places including school, cub scouts, gymnastics practice, soccer practice, etc. Parents should ride with their children for awhile to make sure that they know the way and that they have the skills to handle the bicycle and any problems that may occur. Group family rides are a good way to spend time together and enjoy the outdoors and the scenery. There is evidence indicating that children who learn to enjoy biking and physical activity early in life will probably persist in those activities throughout life. Bicycling is a good activity that children can be successful with at a young age and we think that it is a good habit to start early in life. In most cases, children with various mental and physical handicaps can usually be successful on a bicycle and should be given this opportunity.

MOTIVATING YOURSELF TO USE THE BICYCLE

With the convenience of the car and the many other factors that work against us in regard to starting and maintaining the use of the bicycle, it is important to develop a measure of behavior self-control. Behavior self-control is a systematic procedure that can be used to motivate yourself to develop and maintain specific behavior habits. It uses behavior modification principles that have been verified in many educational settings. We think that beginning cyclists should be aware of these behavioral strategies and use them to help incorporate bicycling into their lifestyle.

Behavior control involves an understanding of the ABC's of behavior modification. The A stands for the antecedent conditions and refers to the conditions when you want the particular behavior to occur. There are many occasions or opportunities for bicycling. This is why we included our discussion on the numerous places and occasions where bicycling is possible. Bicyclers need to decide and schedule the times, places, and situations for bicycling. The B stands for the behavior that you want to control or develop. In this situation, the behavior is simply riding the bicycle. The behavior is clear and straight to the point without any confusion. The C stands for the consequences of riding the bicycle. Some of the consequences are short term and some are long term. Consequences are called reinforcers and they help to control the future behaviors of people. Future bicyclists need to use these ABC's to control their bicycling behavior. We recommend the following strategies for behavior self-control regarding bicycling.

Keep Accurate Records of Bicycling Activities

An extremely important first step in developing a behavior is to record all instances of the behavior. You can record the time that you rode, the distances covered, the specific places that you went, the reasons for going, how you felt afterwards, and your weight. The data can be converted to a daily or weekly graph to show the progress of the biker. For example, you should be able to see a gradual increase in the distances traveled and a reduction in the time that it takes to go various places. You should be able to see an improvement in your physical condition as time passes. Figure 3.2 provides an example of a record-keeping form.

Cycling Record

Date	Time	Place	Weight

Figure 3.2   Record-keeping form

THE **SPORT** EXPERIENCE

> Make up a record-keeping chart and keep track of your bicycling activities for two weeks. Be sure to put the chart in a visible place.

The records and graphs should be kept in a highly visible place so that you will see the data on a regular basis. A good place is on the refrigerator door, a bedroom closet door, or a mirror that is used everyday. When you see the data on a regular basis, it will begin to serve as a discriminative stimulus or cue to remind you of your commitment to cycling. The cue will also remind you to ride the bike at the various times you have scheduled.

These records of gradual improvement in you and your bicycling activities will also serve as regular feedback. You can actually see how you are improving. This serves as reinforcement and motivation for most people. It helps to cause and maintain a behavior change in the desired direction. It keeps people persisting at a particular task.

Schedule Cycling Activities on an Unconditional Basis

There are many demanding priorities that place restraints on our time. Life is usually very busy for most of us. Important bicycling activities must be scheduled into our lifestyle on an unconditional basis. It's a good idea to decide on a set time of the day and a number of days or times per week. You should try to avoid having to cancel any of your bicycling activities. A good approach is to schedule an appointment with yourself for bicycling time. There may be days that you do not feel like keeping your bicycling appointment, but you should try to force yourself because you will probably feel better in the long run. For example, there are days that you do not feel like going to work, taking care of the kids, or mowing the lawn, but they eventually have to be done. Approach your cycling activities the same way.

During the scheduling process of activities, you may want to set some realistic goals for yourself. For example, you may want to ride to work three days per week, ride twenty minutes a night after dinner four times a week, or take a twenty-five mile trip once a month on the week-

Develop a schedule of the cycling activities that you want to do for a two week period and write these down on paper. Read the schedule every day before you go to bed or when you get up in the morning.

end. Your goals can be written and posted so that they can be seen regularly and serve as a constant reminder. These goals should be personal and very minimal to start. It is not important to compare yourself to others and get into a competitive situation with a friend. Cycling should be thought of as a lifelong commitment.

Analyze Troublesome Environmental Factors

After starting your bicycling program, you may find that it is hard to keep on track with the goals or schedule that you have set for yourself. You may need to look carefully at the factors in the environment that are restricting your behavior. The time of day or riding by yourself are examples that may be a problem. Perhaps it is possible to change the time of day or to recruit friends to ride with you. Another example might be that you may need to change your bedtime in order to get up earlier for a morning bicycle ride or you may need to restrict television watching in the evening in order to have enough time for an evening ride. You may want to ride your bicycle on a wind trainer in front of the television set. Many times it is just a matter of changing old habits.

Record the troublesome factors in your life that may conflict with bicycle riding. Discuss these with a friend or teacher to see if you can decide on solutions to the problems.

Establish Positive Consequences for Bicycling

It may take some time for the natural consequences of bicycling to take effect with some individuals. It may be necessary to establish some artificial consequences initially to start you off toward the natural rewards of biking. These artificial rewards need to be meaningful to you. There are many possibilities that may work for you. Some examples are: seeing a new movie, watching a favorite television program, going out for a special dinner, ordering a favorite dessert, buying a new pair of shoes, or buying some new clothes. The rewards could also be very simple, such as taking a hot shower, reading the newspaper, or saying to yourself, "I'm going to look and feel better because of my hard work with this bicycle." These rewards should be attached to specific accomplishments with the bicycle and your physical condition. As your physical conditioning and cycling skills improve, you will probably find that it is not necessary to rely on these artificial rewards anymore and that the natural rewards of cycling will take over.

In the beginning of a bicycling program, it may be necessary to place the reward very close to the bicycling activity. This is a common strategy. After a period of time, you should begin to extend the time between the bicycling activity and the reward system. The rewards should also be harder and harder to acquire as time goes on within the program.

These self-management skills and strategies will help you to become motivated and continue to maintain an appropriate level of enthusiasm for cycling. You should now be ready to work on the specific bicycling skills that will help you to be more comfortable and safe on your bicycle.

BEGINNING CYCLING SKILLS AND LEARNING ACTIVITIES

Now that you have looked at the many ways you can use your bicycle and have learned a little about self-control, you are now ready to start practicing the specific cycling skills. As with any activity, as your skills improve, so will your comfort zone pertaining to the activity. People usually enjoy the activities that they do well. In order to improve your bicycling skills, it is necessary to *practice* these skills. Practice involves some work, time commitment, and energy. We will discuss the skills and give you many practice activities in the following section.

It seems like bicycling skills are simple and that everyone knows how to ride a bike, however, there is a large difference between cycling and cycling well. There are many skills that will improve your proficiency and your ability to cycle safely. A small amount of work with these basic skills will give you a great deal of confidence and comfort in handling your bicycle. The best place to learn is in a deserted parking lot with lots of room to maneuver. Try to avoid the street until you have developed your skills and feel comfortable with your bicycle.

Mounting, Starting, and Stopping

It is a good idea to start riding with a seat that is lower than normal so that you can put your feet flat on the ground or at least close to being flat while seated on the bicycle (see Figure 3.3). After your skills develop, you can raise the seat to a level specified earlier (see Chapter 2). Mounting a bicycle involves the swinging of the foot over the seat and top tube of the frame and ending up in a straddle position over the frame with your hands on the handlebars. Mounting a bike should not occur while walking or running next to the bicycle. Beginners should mount from a stationary position. A moving mount is an advanced skill that will be explained later in the chapter.

Figure 3.3   Starting position

Practice starting and stopping as previously described. Pick out a specific line or spot and practice stopping exactly at that point. Another good practice activity for stopping is to try slowing down to a balanced position without any forward movement before putting your foot on the ground.

Most right-handers will start with the left foot on the ground and the right foot on the pedal at a 2 o'clock position. This position can be reversed if it is more comfortable for you. Try both ways until you are comfortable with one or both positions. If you have toe clips, you must start with one foot in the clip and then slide the opposite foot into the clip while you are moving. Loosen the clips up or even take off the leather straps and bend open the clip before you try this procedure. Starting on a bike involves a simultaneous push off the ground with the ground foot and a push on the pedal with the pedal foot. Your backside will start just in front of the saddle with the front of the saddle slightly touching your backside. As you push off the ground, you will slide back and on to the saddle. As you start pedaling, you may have to adjust your balance and the front tire somewhat until you have the bike under control and rolling smoothly. Try this starting procedure several times until it becomes comfortable and you have a smooth, controlled start.

Stopping involves a gentle squeeze of both brake levers until you slow down enough to slide forward off the saddle placing one foot and then the other foot on the ground. It is important to slow down enough before you try to come off the seat and put your feet down. You can take a fall and hurt yourself if you put your feet down while traveling too fast. Gentle stops should be practiced at a specific point.

Another problem with braking is that you can hurl yourself over the front of your handlebars by squeezing the brakes too hard and too fast. Emergency stopping is a complex skill that will be discussed later in the intermediate skills section. As a beginner, a good general rule is to use the back brake first and the front brake next.

If you feel your back wheel starting to come off the ground during stopping, you are putting too much pressure on the front brake. Start the braking process with the back brake and then start the front brake.

Turning and Changing Levels

A major problem for beginners is to develop turning skills on the bicycle. The key in turning involves the proper amount of body lean. The amount of body lean is determined by the speed of the bicycle, the size of the cyclist, the body position on the bike, and the angle of the turn. Too much body lean can cause the inside pedal to catch on the ground or the bicycle may slip out to the side away from the turn. Beginners also tend to overturn the front wheel during the turn. This skill involves a lot of trial and error with your bike at various speeds and angles. The best way to learn to turn is to simply practice on a variety of obstacles.

THE **SPORT** EXPERIENCE

After you are comfortable with starting and gentle stops, then you can set up an easy obstacle course to practice your turns. The course can be set up with empty pop cans, milk cartons, or any other suitable materials. The course can include circles, figure eights, rectangles, squares, and various other shapes (see Figure 3.4). Practicing should always be done at a slow speed until you begin to become comfortable with the turns. Practice leaning as you make your turns.

Figure 3.4   Tracks for obstacle courses

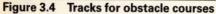

Changing from one level to a higher level surface on a bicycle has caused many beginners and intermediates to take a fall (authors included). What usually happens is that the rider is going too fast and gets the front tire caught on the higher level surface. The momentum of the biker goes toward the higher level and the bike stays at the lower level. This situation can be avoided by making sure that the proper angle is used to approach the higher level. You should attempt to be as close to perpendicular as possible before you make contact with the higher level. If you are riding parallel to the higher level, you must swing your bike out several feet in order to turn and become perpendicular to the higher level. It will also help if you can keep your weight back on your seat and pull up slightly on the handlebars as your front tire hits the higher level. This will help the bike raise up on the higher level. You can save your bike a lot of wear and tear if you can avoid going up over levels that are too high. It is best to stop your bike and simply lift the bike up to the higher level.

Going from a higher level to a lower level such as going off a curb into the street should also be practiced. Most people carry more weight on the rear tire and this can cause broken spokes or, worse yet, a bent rim if the back wheel has to absorb the entire force. The secret is to shift the body weight and the center of gravity to avoid having the wheel taking all of that force. For example, as you go off a curb, you should have your weight back as the front wheel goes off the curb and your weight should shift forward as the rear wheel goes off. This way the weight of your body is off the tire that is coming off the curb. A slower speed will help you to make the weight shift.

THE **SPORT** EXPERIENCE

There are many ways to practice going over different levels. One of the most common places where unlevel surfaces exist is from the street surface to a driveway that has a two-to-four inch raised surface. These are good practice areas if you pick one that does not have much auto traffic. You can practice making turns at various angles and speeds until you are comfortable. The first few turns should be done at a very slow speed. You should check the areas where you are going to be riding and keep your eyes open for unlevel areas. Other possibilities might include street curbs, railroad tracks, streetcar tracks, sewer gratings where you are sure the holes are smaller than your tires, cattle guards, and drainage areas on the side of the road.

Avoiding Bumps, Potholes, and Road Hazards

There are many road hazards that will make riding difficult and uncomfortable. It is nice if you can avoid all of these but it will probably be impossible. There are several skills that you can practice in order to improve the comfort of your rides and help to save repairs to your bicycle. The first skill that you can work on is to learn to read the road carefully and decide on a plan of attack as to which hazards you can avoid and which you will have to ride through carefully. It involves getting into the habit of looking ahead and being alert to possible obstacles. When you have time to make decisions, you can make a series of slow, smooth turns. If you come upon unexpected hazards too quickly, it may be possible to make several quick turns to avoid obstacles. These quick turns can be made with a slight pulling action with your handlebars to one side and then quickly back to the original position without moving off the original line of travel. You have to remember that you are using a two-wheel track and that you have to miss the hazards with both the front and back wheels. This maneuver can be practiced at a slow speed with artificial hazards that will not wreck the bike in the event that you hit one.

When it is necessary to ride over large elevated bumps, you will want to use the pull-up procedure briefly talked about in the section on

Figure 3.5   Pull-up procedure

Practice the pull-up procedure in a school parking lot or factory parking lot that has lots of speed bumps. The weekends or early morning are good times to find these areas vacant.

uneven surfaces (see Figure 3.5). It involves shifting your weight back and up as you pull up the handlebars at the instant when the front wheel hits the obstacle. Proper timing and coordination are important in executing this skill.

Another common technique that you will use for riding over bumps is to raise up off of your saddle with your pedals in a parallel position to the ground. A large portion of your weight will be carried on the arms. As you hit the bumps, allow the arms and legs to bend and give with the upward motion of the bicycle. This enables the arms, legs, and knees to serve as shock absorbers.

Looking Back and Signaling

Another important beginning skill is to be able to look backward while riding and keep the bicycle going in a straight line. It is necessary to look back before turning, changing lanes, and keeping aware of the traffic flow. It is easy to get off course while looking back and being off course can cause an unnecessary accident. We recommend that you sit up and look over your left shoulder and take your left hand off the handlebars. The right hand should be moved slightly toward the center stem of the handlebars. The bicycle should be controlled with the right hand only. You must concentrate on keeping the bike on a straight line (see Figure 3.6).

If you are riding in traffic and want to stay in the lower position on a dropped handlebar, it is possible to look back over your left shoulder without taking either hand off of the handlebars. The problem is that you have a tendency to steer into traffic as you are looking back. You just need to practice this skill and concentrate on keeping the bike on a straight course. Some skilled riders will even look back through the space between the left arm and the body. This skill requires more

Incorporating Cycling into Your Lifestyle

Figure 3.6 Looking backwards

practice and offers only a limited view but it can be used if it is necessary to stop quickly.

Hand signaling is a very important safety skill for cyclists. These signals are similar to those used with the automobile. They can be used with right and left turns as well as for stopping. There are two separate signals for the right turn (see Figures 3.7, 3.8, 3.9, 3.10). These signals should be practiced so that the bike can be controlled with one hand while signaling. The bicycle must be maintained in a straight line during the signaling process. An important technique in signaling is to try

A good practice activity for these skills is to find an isolated area with a painted line on the street and see if you can follow the line while looking backward using the techniques that we have suggested. You should also practice these techniques while looking back to the left and to the right.

Figure 3.7 Right turn signal (left arm bent upward)   **Figure 3.8 Right turn signal (right arm extended)**

Figure 3.9 Left turn signal   **Figure 3.10 Stopping signal**

making yourself as visible as possible by sitting up tall and waving your arm a little to make sure that everyone sees you and understands in which direction you will be traveling. Hand signals are a method of communication and you need to be quite clear to those people around you. Make your decisions about turning and communicate them clearly.

Body and Hand Positions on the Bicycle

If you have a bicycle that has some type of raised handlebars, you will have to ride in an upright position with your hands on the grips (see Figure 3.11). These types of handlebars force you to ride in this position which is comfortable and safe for touring and relatively short rides.

If you have a bike with dropped handlebars, there are several body and hand positions you will want to master while you are learning to cycle. There is much disagreement on which riding position is the most efficient, most comfortable, and the safest. Each position has advan-

Figure 3.11   Upright riding position— raised handlebars

Figure 3.12   Dropped position— dropped handlebars

Figure 3.13   Lowest grip on dropped handlebars

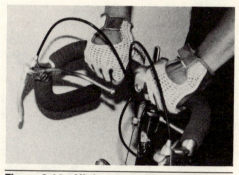

Figure 3.14   Highest grip on dropped handlebars

tages and disadvantages. The position you choose should be related to the goals that you have in mind and the position that is most comfortable for you. We think that you should try all of them and use a variety of positions throughout your rides. However, you should be aware that if you are going to be using your bike for long distances at a fast speed, you will want to ride in a dropped position (see Figure 3.12). The dropped position is aerodynamically sound and will get you out of the wind. It takes longer to become comfortable with the dropped position and you cannot watch the scenery as well as in the upright position.

It is possible to ride in an upright position even with dropped handlebars. This is a comfortable position that allows you to see the scenery and enjoy your environment more than the dropped position. A key to riding comfortably with dropped handlebars is to master the variety of hand positions. There are four basic hand positions.

The lowest grip (see Figure 3.13) is good for getting as low as possible and out of a headwind. It is hard to see as much scenery from this position. However, it is best for speed. It can also be good for high traffic situations because you have quick access to your brakes. Many people feel that the highest grip (see Figure 3.14) on the top of the bars is the most comfortable for the neck, seat, and back. This grip is also good for climbing hills if the hands are kept as far apart as possible. A problem with this grip is that the narrow base of the hands can affect your balance. There is also poor access to the brakes unless you have the auxiliary brake levers that extend up to the upper part of the handlebars. Be sure that you are aware that the auxiliary levers are not as effective and can be dangerous.

Figure 3.15 Intermediate grip on dropped handlebars (hands on the brake hoods)

Figure 3.16 Intermediate grip on dropped handlebars (hands on the curve of the handlebar)

The two intermediate grips (see Figures 3.15 and 3.16) are in between the upper and lower grips. The grip with the hands on the hoods of the brakes allows easier access to the brakes and can be good for hill climbing. The grip with the hands slightly above the brake hoods and on the sides of the handlebars will allow easier steering and better balance. Many experienced cyclists think that this intermediate grip is the most comfortable and is good for flat areas as well as hilly areas. By varying your grip it is possible to reduce the stress on the arms, wrists, neck, etc., and to have a more comfortable ride. We have found that no matter what grip you use, it is necessary to continually bend your arms slightly at the elbow to release the pressure on the hands. The hands and fingers can go numb during long rides because of pressure on the ulnar nerve. Grips and body positions have to be tested by each per-

THE **SPORT** EXPERIENCE

A good practice activity is to ride with one hand and keep the bike on a painted line on the pavement without deviating more than a few inches (see Figure 3.17).

Figure 3.17   One-handed riding on a line

Incorporating Cycling into Your Lifestyle

son because each body type and size will affect the individual's riding comfort zone.

Another body and grip position that is a good idea to practice is riding with one hand because of the numerous times that it becomes necessary during signaling, looking back, shifting gears, drinking water, and so on. We do not recommend riding with one hand on a regular basis but it should be practiced because it is necessary at times. Riding with one hand involves moving the hand on the handlebars closer to the stem in order to provide a little more stability. The balance of the bike is also slightly different and gives the rider a different feel that should be practiced. You should practice riding with either hand on the handlebar so that you are comfortable riding with either hand.

INTERMEDIATE AND ADVANCED SKILLS AND LEARNING ACTIVITIES

After practicing and developing the skills included in the beginning level section, you are now ready to move into the intermediate and advanced level skills. These skills will enhance your enjoyment of the bicycle because you will be able to do more and different kinds of bicycling activities. Remember to work on them at your own pace and take your time because you have a lifetime to use and enjoy them.

Moving Mount

The moving mount is performed by placing the left foot on the left pedal and the right foot on the ground behind the left pedal. The hands are placed on the handlebars in the upright position. You push off the ground with the ground foot and after you gain a little speed and balance, you swing the right foot over the seat and top tube until it lands on the right pedal. Your backside should land on the seat. You can start from the opposite side of the bicycle with your feet reversed if you prefer.

Toe Clips for Efficiency

The use of toe clips will help to keep the ball of the foot centered over the pedal and thus will enhance the efficiency of the rider. The pedaling efficiency is enhanced because the foot will not slip around on the pedal and will always be in the best position for the downstroke of the pedaling revolution. The toe clips also allow the rider to slightly lift the pedal during the upstroke. This gives you an effective combination of pushing down and pulling up. Toe clips initially are uncomfortable and seem to be more trouble than they are worth. However, most people that make the effort to get used to them will swear by them after a period of time. There is really no problem with getting the feet out of the clips in an emergency situation if you understand how they work and do not keep the straps too tight in traffic situations. The foot comes out of the toe clip backward and not sideways. When you are biking on the open road with less traffic, you may want to tighten up the straps slightly.

When you begin to use your toe clips, it is a good idea to remove the toe straps and just use the clips. From a starting position, place one foot in the toe clip and push off the ground with the opposite foot. It is probably best to take three or four pedal strokes to gain some speed and balance. With your unclipped foot, you must then flip the toe clip up into a position so that you can slide your foot forward into the clip. While you are doing this, you must keep the bike going and straight on course. If you are having problems, you may want to reach down and put your foot into position until you gain better control with your feet. The opening of the clip needs to be wide enough to slide your foot in without catching on the top shoestrings of your shoe. This is a common problem. Be sure to practice in an isolated area where you will not hit anything.

After you feel comfortable with this procedure, then you can add the toe straps. Be sure to look carefully and adjust the release mechanism on the straps so that you can tighten or loosen them quickly while riding. Start practicing with the straps as loose as possible and slowly tighten them up. We recommend that you keep the straps fairly loose in any kind of traffic. Practice stopping quickly and sliding the foot out. Practice getting into the clips enough so that you can do it without looking at the pedals at all. Keep your eyes on the road straight ahead. The key to effectively using toe clips is understanding how they work and practice using them.

Shifting

With a standard 3-speed bicycle, shifting is really a simple beginning level skill. We have included it in the intermediate section because shifting with a 10-speed derailleur system requires much more skill and practice than with the 3-speed. If you are using a standard 3-speed bike, shifting simply involves the moving of the shift lever while the bike is stopped or moving. When the bike is moving, it is necessary to stop pedaling during the shift. One advantage of the 3-speed is that the gears can be shifted at a stop sign or stoplight while the 10-speed must be shifted while in motion. Obviously, the 3-speed does not offer the range of gears for various terrains.

As you know from Chapter 2, there are many different derailleur systems, shifting levers, and places where they are attached to various 10-speed bicycles. You will have to become comfortable with the arrangement on your bike or change the system to the one you prefer. Many people have different ideas about which one is best for different situations. As to which arrangement is best for you, it is best to remember our earlier discussion on what type of bicycling you will be doing most of the time. Whichever derailleur system you have, there are several general shifting techniques that you should practice and master.

If you are just learning about shifting and gears on a 10-speed bicycle, you should try to get an idea of how the system works by having one or two people help you. Since it is necessary to be pedaling while you are shifting, one person must hold up the seat and lift the back tire off the ground while the other person turns the pedals. While this is taking place, you can be slowly shifting the levers to get the feel of your system. Move your shift levers for both the front and rear derailleurs to make sure that they are working properly. You should be able to move the chain smoothly through the full range of gears.

Shifting is a skill that involves sound and feel. As you move the shift levers, you will be able to hear the derailleur making contact with the chain and movement of the chain from gear to gear. You will also be able to feel the pressure change on the pedals. The pressure that you put on your particular shift lever causes the derailleur and chain to respond in the manner that you desire. These sounds and pressures are very subtle. As you practice and become comfortable with your system, the sound and feel will help you to make smooth, even changes of the gears.

The rear derailleur is a bit more difficult to shift because there are usually five or six cogs that can be used whereas the front derailleur usually offers two choices. The smaller cogs will give you a higher gear and the larger cogs are the lower gears. A little practice and you will soon be able to feel the difference. It is harder to get the chain to stop exactly on the cog that you want. Many times you will overshift by

There are several key points in learning to shift smoothly. The first step is to find a quiet, isolated, flat area where you can practice. Remember to start slowly and be very gentle with your shift levers as you begin. It is best to start practicing with the front derailleur because it usually only has two chainrings. The shifting process simply moves the chain from the large ring to the small ring and back again. As you start to shift, you must remember to ease up on the pressure on the pedals while still pedaling. Then you pull the shift lever back to upshift or push it forward to downshift. Practice with the front derailleur until you can get a smooth, even shift. Start with the chain on the large ring in the front and the middle cog on the rear. Move the chain back and forth five times.

going past the cog that you desire or undershift by not going far enough. It is necessary to gently ease the shift lever forward or backward to move the chain into the various gears. Remember to keep pedaling but ease off slightly on the pressure on the pedals. If you are pedaling too hard during the shifting process, you may jump past the cogs too quickly and actually damage the cogs. Of course, there will be some grinding or clinking noise during any shift so do not be overly alarmed.

One common problem with shifting is that if you have to park in a public area, someone may tamper with your shift levers while the bike is parked. This can cause you problems when you start to bike because you may be in-between gears and when you start up, you will get an unexpected slip to a smaller cog. Damage to your cogs or to your body can occur if you are not expecting the change in gears. If you have a bike with shift levers on the ends of dropped handlebars, this same problem can happen if your bike is bumped or if it falls in some way that causes the levers to be moved. It is a good habit to carefully check your shift levers and the position of your chain each time that you get on your bike.

Regarding the usage of your gears, we recommend that you experiment with your bike over the terrain that you will normally be riding

A common problem with shifting is that you may hear a slight rubbing or grinding noise after you have shifted.

This usually means that you need to slightly adjust the shift lever to properly line up the derailleur with the chain so that they do not rub. Just move the shift lever slightly forward or backward and the noise should stop.

Another problem during shifting is that your chain may not drop on any cog and your pedals just spin around.

This probably means that you will have to adjust the shift lever again to get the chain to drop.

Another annoying problem with shifting is when the chain slips out of gear after you have shifted.

This can be corrected by tightening the shift lever. You will have to experiment with the tightness because the lever can be too tight and, consequently, too hard to shift. If the lever is too loose, it will continue to slip out of gear.

THE **SPORT**
EXPERIENCE

Start with the chain on the small front chainring and middle cog in the back. As you pick up speed, shift to the large front chainring and stay in this position until you come to a stoplight. Before stopping, downshift to the small front chainring and then repeat this procedure. Obviously, if you ride over hilly terrain, you will have to use your gears more often than over flat terrain. The wind will also be another factor that will have to be considered.

and read the next section on cadence to help you make decisions about what is comfortable for you in each situation. A good starting procedure is to put the back derailleur so that the chain is on the middle cog and then do your shifting with only the front chainrings.

Cadence

Pedaling cadence refers to the speed in which you pedal your bike. It is expressed in revolutions per minute (rpm). Most experienced and effective cyclists try to maintain the same cadence while riding except for large hills where it is necessary to slow down the cadence. Constant cadence is maintained by shifting gears. For example, as you begin to slow down because of a headwind, a small hill, or because you just become tired, you need to shift to a lower gear so that the same cadence is maintained. When you speed up because of a tailwind or when you are going downhill, you will need to shift to a higher gear. By keeping a constant cadence, you will conserve energy and become a more efficient cyclist.

Most beginners tend to pedal too slowly because they feel that it is necessary to push against some resistance and they are not comfort-

THE SPORT EXPERIENCE

There are several ways to develop the feel of a particular cadence. As you begin to pedal and gain an even speed, look at the second hand of your watch or use a stopwatch and begin counting every time one foot goes past the bottom arc of each revolution of the pedal. Stop counting after 30 seconds and multiply by two or count for 15 seconds and multiply by four. If you are not able to maintain a cadence that you have selected, you need to shift to a lower gear. The opposite problem is when you cannot keep up with the pedals, you will need a higher gear. Be sure to remember that hills and the wind will affect your cadence. It is best to practice cadence on the flat ground without the wind.

Try to start each pedaling revolution with a smooth, even exertion of force on the downstroke, then a pulling backward feeling at the bottom of the stroke, and follow this with a smooth lifting action during the upstroke. It is possible to concentrate on each pedaling revolution during practice sessions. After a while, smooth pedaling should become part of your comfort zone.

able with pedaling fast. We recommend that you try to shoot for a cadence of 70–80 rpms while you are learning. After a while of working at the 70–80 rpm range, most cyclists start to increase the cadence to 80–90 rpms. Most expert cyclists will maintain a cadence in the 100–120 rpm range. As we have said throughout this book, cycling should be comfortable for you if you are going to become a lifetime addict. Try the various cadence ranges and pick one that you enjoy.

Another skill that you can work on in conjunction with cadence is the technique of pedaling. Efficient pedaling is accomplished by trying to maintain a smooth, circular arc with the pedals. Too many riders use short, choppy surges for pedaling. This is wasted energy and causes fatigue too early for the cyclist.

Emergency Braking

An extremely important but dangerous biking skill is the emergency or panic stop. Inevitably, we all must be able to stop quickly in certain situations. Since the front brakes have almost double the stopping power of the back brakes, it is necessary to exert a powerful force on the front brakes and a lighter force on the back brakes. There are a couple of key points in developing this skill. If you start to feel the back wheel skidding, then you must immediately release the pressure on the front brakes. When the back wheel starts to skid, it is ready to lift up off the ground and throw you over the top of the handlebars. It is important to release the brakes in order to maintain traction. It is also necessary to keep the front wheel straight during the stop to help keep the rear wheel down.

This stopping procedure can be practiced by riding at a slow speed in an isolated area. Start to pedal until you are moving slowly and then squeeze the front brake forcefully until the back wheel actually starts to come off the ground. As soon as this happens, release the pressure until the bike comes down under control. Practice this technique until you have a feel or reflex for the proper time to ease the pressure on the front brake. Be sure to practice with both hands working on the brakes and keeping the weight back on the rear of the saddle. If you have practiced this skill at a slow speed, you will have a better chance to control your bike when you have to make an emergency stop in a real situation.

Riding in Traffic

The first several experiences for a beginning rider in heavy traffic can be quite nervewracking. Cars and trucks are bearing down on you from the left side and people are opening the doors of their parked cars into your path from the right. It can be a frustrating and dangerous situation if you are not careful. Biking in traffic should be a combination of offensive and defensive strategies. There are many areas of concern but it should still be an enjoyable experience.

One of the first things to remember is that you have the same rights and obligations as the operators of those large, heavy vehicles called cars. You must follow the same rules and regulations they are supposed to follow. As you well know, there are always plenty of car operators and cyclists who do not follow the rules. Some cyclists will even ignore stop signs, traffic lights, or ride on the wrong side of the street. When we see a cyclist riding on the wrong side right toward us, we try to wave him to the correct side. Anyway, you must take care of your riding behavior before you try to change that of others.

When you ride in traffic, you should make yourself as visible as possible (see Chapter 4). Since you are traveling at a slower speed, you must make your intentions clear so that others have time to react to you. As you change lanes, make turns, or approach intersections, you

The problem with using the front brake for an emergency stopping procedure is that the front wheel can lock and cause you to flip over the front of the handlebars. If you are going downhill or have too much weight forward on the bike, this will also compound the problem. The secret of this technique is to apply the back brake lightly as the front brake is forcefully utilized. At the same time, you must slide your weight back on the saddle (see Figure 3.18).

Figure 3.18   Emergency braking position

need to signal clearly and use eye contact to assert yourself. You must be aware that you are on a vehicle that is smaller than what other drivers are used to seeing and that it is possible to miss seeing a cyclist if you are not clearly visible. This is why we recommend that you make an extra wave of your signals, sit a bit taller when approaching a potentially dangerous situation, and wear colorful clothing.

We recommend that you choose your riding routes so that there are less cars and probably slower speeds by the traffic. Streets that have bicycle paths, wide areas, and less traffic are most enjoyable for us. Other cyclists prefer to ride the main arteries because they can travel at a faster speed. There are usually less traffic lights and better roads. This is something that you can decide. The choice of routes is an important decision especially in heavy traffic areas.

When you are riding in the traffic, you do have the right to use as much of the street that you think is necessary to be safe. You may have to use your position on the road to assert yourself. Be offensive but be prepared for a defensive action if necessary. Do not get forced too far over to the right so that you are off the road into the dirt shoulder. Give yourself enough room with parked cars on the right. Always assume that someone may be opening one of the doors. When you are going through an intersection, always be aware of cars that might be making a right turn into you or just in front of you. Do not try to make a right turn on the inside of a car that is also turning right because you can get squeezed off the road. You may be in a blind spot for the driver of the car. Left turns are more dangerous than right turns because you may have to cross in front of traffic. You need to signal and get over into the turning lane. Stay in the middle of the turning lane so that you can keep cars behind you and you can easily get over to the right side of the road after you make the turn. Be careful with the speed of the oncoming traffic. If you cannot get into the left turning lane because of the volume of traffic, you can go through the intersection and stop at the corner and cross with the traffic when the light changes. Some cyclists call this the Big Left Turn or the European Crossing. It is slower but safer and may be necessary at times.

Hill Climbing

Hill climbing can be a challenging, enjoyable experience or an agonizing, painful experience. Some riders will even try to avoid hills, while others will seek them out. We think that hills should be considered a challenge to your biking skill with gears, cadence, and body position. It's all a matter of your attitude about hill climbing. In most cases, you will probably have little choice as to whether you want to ride them or avoid them. Hills will certainly be a challenge to your fitness level. Gains in physical fitness can certainly be made if you do a lot of hill work on your bike.

Whether you are climbing hills in heavy traffic or on a rural road, there are several skills that you can practice. Hill climbing can be dangerous because you have to slow to such a low speed. It is necessary to stay as far right as possible because the cars will be speeding by you. Keep a good check on the traffic flow behind you. It is a good idea to make an extra effort to keep yourself visible by waving the cars on with your arm. If you know that you will be riding a lot of hills during a particular day, you should make sure that you wear your most visible clothes and equipment. You also have to be concerned with keeping the bike straight and off the shoulder as you are straining to keep up an even cadence. The bike will tend to weave and wander on the road as you get tired.

Gearing, cadence, and body position are important for hill climbing. The size and length of the hill will have an effect on your gears and cadence. If the hill is new to you, it is best to shift to a lower gear early because it is easier to get into a higher gear if you find that you can not keep up with the pedals. You have to find a good rhythm for you on each hill. Some people can keep a faster cadence in a lower gear while others can keep low cadence in a higher gear. It depends on your strength and fitness level. You should experiment with various gears and cadence on hills.

You will want to practice coming out of the saddle into a standing position for climbing (see Figure 3.19). This position adds power to your stroke even though it costs you more energy. Most bikers will climb hills by riding some on the saddle and some out of the saddle. Again, this is something that you can practice and experiment with on different-size hills. As you stand, your hand position should be on the top of the hoods of the brakes. It is not necessary to ride in the lower position on the drops because of the slow speed. You should bring your body position slightly forward and pull with your arms on the handlebars in conjunction with each push on the pedals. Make sure that you keep your center of gravity over the bottom bracket so that you will not lose important power. The body will sway slightly to each side as you are pushing and pulling. The bike and your body can sway laterally but make sure that the bike stays in a straight line on the road. Pedaling should have a definite push on the downstroke and a lift on the upstroke.

Long hills mean a tiring ride and you should plan on shifting several times. As your cadence slows, go to a lower gear that is comfortable. Try to make your shifts early enough to keep the same cadence. It is also good to regularly change positions of the arms on the handlebars to reduce the onset of fatigue. Many riders will also change their body positions several times during a long hill. It is possible for a beginner to run out of energy on a long hill. You may have to get off and walk for

Figure 3.19   Standing position for hills

a while. Stay to the right of your bike and get as far off the road as you think is safe.

A problem that exists at the top of the hill and just over the top is that cars will have less time to see you than normally is available. You may be invisible for a slight period of time. This is an especially important time to stay as far to the right as possible and be listening for traffic from behind. Do not slide into the middle of your lane for any reason. Try to stay as visible as possible with an upright position and a swaying head or motioning arm. As you pick up speed on the downhill side, you may find yourself gaining on cars. Remember to avoid getting too close because you do not have the same braking capabilities as a car. If there is not a lot of traffic, you may want to ease out from the right side to give yourself more room to maneuver in case of turns or rough surfaces on the road. The increase in speed means that you should try to get as much room as is safe in the situation. You may want to get down on the drops closer to the brake levers and slide your weight back on the saddle.

You have to learn the difference between wide and narrow roads in regard to where you can position yourself in the right lane. Your position is determined by visibility and the ability of cars to pass each other and you safely on a narrow road. This refers not only to hill situations, but also to flat roads.

MISCELLANEOUS ADVANCED SKILLS

Balancing

A challenging, fun activity to try on your bike is to practice balancing in one spot without moving forward. It involves keeping the bike in a balanced upright position without pedaling forward. Have someone time you with a stopwatch so that you can keep track of how long you can stay balanced. The best place to practice this skill is in a wide, flat area such as an empty parking lot. Give yourself a seven to eight yard flat area where you can practice the skill. Start pedaling and then slow yourself down to almost a full stop in the designated balance area. You will have to move the front wheel and lean from side to side in order to maintain your balance. Many advanced riders using toe clips with cleated shoes can be seen balancing at a stoplight because they do not want to stop and put their foot down.

Riding with No Hands

Riding with no hands is a skill that can come in handy when you are riding and need to use both hands for putting on a rain poncho, un-wrapping a hamburger, or pulling off a shirt. It can be quite dangerous if you are not careful and hit something in the road. We recommend that you practice this skill under careful conditions so that if you have to use it on the open road, you will be comfortable with it. The skill involves sitting back in the saddle in an upright position and steering the bicycle by shifting your body position on the saddle. While you are practicing, keep your hands ready to quickly grab the handlebars in case you lose control. After practicing, you will probably find that you can control the bike relatively well with no hands. We do not recommend riding with no hands on a regular basis. There are usually too many roads that are uneven and will cause you to lose control.

Cleaning Your Tires

Another skill that you may want to get in the habit of using is to wipe off your tires after running over some glass on the road. It may save you a flat tire or two if you learn this skill. It is better to wipe off broken glass while you are riding rather than braking to a stop. The longer that the glass is on the tire, the greater the chance that some of the glass will get imbedded in the tire tread and will eventually work its way to the tube. Mud is another substance that you will want to get off the tires. Some bikers will use their foot to apply light pressure on either the front or back wheel. The key is to stop pedaling and slowly ease the foot closer to the wheel until you make contact with the mud or glass. You must be careful to keep the foot away from the spokes and from putting too much pressure and getting the foot caught in the front fork or the frame on the back.

If you wear biking gloves, you can wipe the tires with the glove while riding. This technique is safe if you are careful and practice the skill. The front wheel is the easiest because you can see it well and can reach down in front of the brake and slowly apply pressure until the material is gone. You need to lean forward, keep your balance, and slowly bring the palm of the hand in contact with the tire for several revolutions. The rear tire is more tricky because it is harder to see. You must be careful to put your hand between the seat tube and the rear seat stays. The thumb should be hooked around the seat stay with the palm down and centered over the tire. Slowly lower the hand until it brushes off the material. Be careful with this and practice at a slow speed until you are comfortable. If you are not comfortable with this technique, then do not use it. Just stop the bike and clean the tires after you are off the road.

Jumping

If you ride a cruiser or a mountain bike, there may be opportunities for you to actually jump over small objects on or off the road. We do not recommend trying to jump with a normal 10-speed bike because the rims were not made for jumping and you could break some spokes or bend a rim. Jumping is an extension of the pull-up procedure for getting up to a higher level surface that was discussed earlier in the chapter. We recommend that you go back and reread that section.

Jumping involves a combination of speed and a pulling up on the handlebars and pedals at the right instant. The pulling-up procedure with the handlebars and pedals can be done at the same time if you have toe clips on your feet. If you do not have toe clips, then you push off the pedals and bring the bike up while using your arms and the handlebars all in one motion. You need to think of going up as one unit. In order to be effective, the speed factor must be considered because if you are not going fast enough, you will go up and then come down on the target because the bike is too long. It is necessary to practice at different speeds and heights so that you can get a feel for the proper momentum and how high you can actually get the bike off the ground. Be sure to use your helmet and other pads during your practice sessions and start low with a small stick on a couple of rocks.

Figure 3.20   Wheelie position

Some people even try jumping sideways to get up on a curb or over an obstacle on the side. It is the same technique as the straight ahead jump except that you jump and shift your weight sideways. Do not try to go too high or too far laterally. It is necessary to get as close as possible to the target that you want to jump on or over. You want to land as close to perpendicular as possible with the wheels straight ahead. This is a difficult skill that we do not recommend for everyone.

Wheelies

Another advanced skill that you may want to try on a cruiser or mountain bike is a wheelie. The skill involves balancing on the rear wheel with the front wheel in the air. Your center of gravity must be moved backwards over the rear wheel. It is necessary to get the bike moving and then lift the front wheel up and back until you are in a balanced position. Some skilled riders can ride in a wheelie position for a long period of time. The key is to practice slowly until you have a sense of balance in the wheelie position (see Figure 3.20).

In summary, this chapter has given you many ideas about how to use your bicycle and ways to make cycling a part of your lifestyle. There are many skills to bicycling and many ways to practice these skills. Practice the skills that will be most useful to you and enjoy your bicycle.

Bicycle Safety

Safety is simply a matter of common sense. However, safety can be planned and practiced. It is best to remember that when a car and a bicycle tangle, the bicycle rider is always the loser. One of the authors of this book spent four days in a hospital after being hit from behind by a car. He now always uses a mirror and knows when cars are approaching from behind. This is an example of how equipment can add to your safety when bicycling. An example of equipment that could cause an accident is radio headsets. If headsets are used they should be kept on a very low volume. We also recommend that radio headsets not be used when riding in traffic. Bicycle safety includes (1) proven safety equipment, (2) good bicycle maintenance, (3) following bicycling rules, and (4) practice on safety rules.

BICYCLE SAFETY EQUIPMENT

Bicycle safety equipment includes all of the auxiliary equipment that is attached to the bicycle or worn by the rider for safety.

Helmets

Probably the number-one piece of safety equipment for a serious bicycle rider is a good helmet. Some people will say that the helmet is not necessary, and one would hope that the helmet is never needed. However, if a bicyclist should be involved in a serious accident, the helmet may save his or her life. We consider the helmet for the bike equivalent to the seat belt for the car. You may get in the habit of not wearing the helmet if you are just going down the block to the store. However, you must remember that most accidents occur close to home.

Most people who own helmets and do not wear them on short trips use the same excuse as the driver who does not put on his or her seatbelt for a short trip. Yet accidents occur everywhere—on long trips and on short trips. If you put your helmet on your bicycle seat when you are not riding your bicycle, you will always remember to wear your helmet. You will be forced to pick it up and the best place to put the helmet is on your head. So get in the habit of putting your helmet on your bicycle seat. Of course, we are assuming you will keep your bicycle in a safe place when not riding and no one will steal your helmet. If you can't keep your bicycle in a safe place then you will want to lock your helmet to the bicycle.

There are several types of helmets currently on the market (see Figure 4.1). All of them have some good and bad points. Some helmets have better ventilation than others. If you live and ride in a hot part of the country, a well-ventilated helmet is a must. Of course, you will give up a little protection for a better ventilated helmet. Talk to your local bicycle club for information about the type of helmet that is best for the area in which you live. You will find that the local bicycle clubs have a lot of information concerning helmets and where to buy them.

Figure 4.1   Examples of helmets

Figure 4.2   Examples of mirrors

Mirrors

The second piece of safety equipment that you should invest in for your bicycle is a mirror. The mirror will tell you where other bicycles and cars are in relationship to your back. Riding a bicycle in traffic or on streets without a mirror would be like driving a car that had no rear-view mirror. It may be possible, but it is a lot safer to have the mirror. It is extremely important to know where other vehicles are at all times. Many bicycle/car accidents occur when cars making right turns plow into bicycles. The car driver does not see the bicycle and the bicycle rider is not aware that a car is approaching from the rear. By having a mirror, the bicyclist might avoid this type of accident. Bicycle mirrors can be mounted on the handlebar or clipped on the helmet (see Figure 4.2).

Lights and Reflectors

If you plan on riding your bicycle at night or at dusk, lights and reflectors are a must for safe bicycling. Lights and reflectors are required by most states when riding at night. Headlights should project a white light that is visible from a distance of 500 or more feet. Red taillights should also project up to 500 or more feet. When buying lights for your bicycle, a decision between battery-run lights or generator-run lights must be made. Both lighting systems have advantages and disadvantages.

The biggest disadvantage of generator-run lights is the lack of lights when the bicycle is not moving. The generator only produces power when the bicycle wheel is turning, and there is only light when the generator is producing power. Cheap generators also have a tendency to produce poor lighting when the bicycle is not moving very fast. This is not a problem with better generators that, of course, cost more. It should be noted that the new, more expensive generator sets also come with halogen lights and produce a very bright light that can be seen for more than 500 feet even with low power output. These generator sets sell for about $20 to $30.

The battery-run light does not go out when the bicycle is at a stop. The battery-run light stays on all the time. The major disadvantage of the battery-run light is that batteries run down (it seems they run down just when you need them the most). As the battery runs down, the light gets dimmer and dimmer until you cannot see the 500 feet required by most state laws. If you do not use lights often you will not know what condition your battery is in, and will be surprised to find out you do not have lights. Batteries can run down just from sitting in a flashlight. Of course, if you have a generator light you will always have lights that work without batteries.

Many bicyclists will not ride with light generators because they claim that the generator slows them down. Since the generator does rub against the wheel, creating friction, they have a point. However, if you buy a good generator set, the amount of power lost to running the light will not be noticeable. The authors of this book feel the reliability

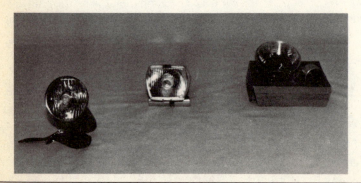

Figure 4.3   Examples of lighting systems

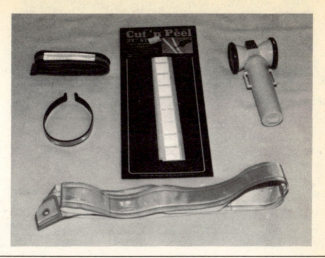

Figure 4.4   Reflective material and T-light

of the generator versus the battery light is a major consideration when buying a lighting system (see Figure 4.3 for examples).

Safety Clothing

If you ride at night or in heavy traffic you want auto drivers to see you. One of the best ways to draw attention to yourself is to wear clothing that will catch the eye of the driver. There are several types of fluorescent vests on the market that drivers can see very easily. They come in several colors and are easy to slip over most jackets or shirts. You can also buy flexible pole-mounted bicycle flags that make the bicycle much more noticeable to other vehicles and bicyclists. The major problem with pole flags is that they can hamper the leg over-the-saddle mount. Many bicyclists will wear a T-light (this light is battery run—see Figure 4.4). The T-light has a white lens on one end of the T and a red lens on the other side of the T. The T-light can be worn on the leg or arm. If the light is worn on the leg below the knee it has a circular pattern due to the pedaling action and is very noticeable to the motorist. However, this is only a supplemental light and should never replace a proper front and rear light.

Safety Equipment on Parked Bicycles

Go to a place where a lot of bicycles are parked, such as a high school, junior high school, elementary school, park, college, etc. Examine the parked bicycles and see if you can spot any of the following safety equipment:

1. lights
2. reflectors
3. baskets and carriers
4. mirrors
5. horns or bells
6. pole flags
7. other equipment used for safety

Count the number of bicycles parked and then place a checkmark next to each of the above items for each bicycle. Then answer the following questions:

1. What was the most common piece of safety equipment on the bicycles?
2. What piece of safety equipment did you not see?
3. Do you think the age of the bicycle rider makes a difference in the type of safety equipment found (high school versus elementary school)?

Safety Equipment at the Bicycle Shop

Go to a local bicycle shop: look around at the type of safety equipment included on their bicycles. Notice and complete the following questions and activities:

1. What safety equipment is on the used bicycles?
2. What safety equipment is on the new bicycles?
3. Talk to a person who works in the shop about safety equipment.

4. Investigate the type of helmets the shop sells.
5. Ask the clerk for an opinion of each helmet.
6. Ask the clerk about lighting systems (battery or generator).

Safety Equipment on Moving Bicycles

As you walk or drive around town notice the types of safety equipment you see on moving bicycles. Answer the following questions:

1. Do most bicycle riders use lights at night?
2. How easy are bicycles to see at night?
3. Do most bicycle riders use helmets?

Horns, Bells, Carriers, and Other Equipment

Horns or bells are another piece of safety equipment that many cyclists buy. They are useful when riding on sidewalks or bike paths to warn pedestrians and other bicyclists that you are behind them. Many people feel that the bell and horn are intrusive and do not use them. The bell has less of a jolt to the nervous system than the horn. We recommend the bell over the horn. The bell is a nicer way to warn people and does not create negative feelings like the horn.

Chain guards are helpful in keeping pant cuffs out of the chain. If you do not want to buy a chain guard, you can buy small spring clamps or straps that go around the cuff. The clamps or straps do an excellent job of keeping the cuff off the chain and also help keep the cuff from getting greasy. If your cuff gets caught in the chain it can lead to a nasty fall or can cause the rider to swerve into traffic.

Carriers are a necessary safety item if you plan on carrying any articles. Avoid putting large or heavy packages on the front of the bicycle. When large front baskets are loaded they cause steering problems. Therefore, it is best not to have large front baskets. See Chapter 2 for more information concerning carriers.

If you choose to ride with toe clips, be sure that at least one foot can be removed quickly from the clip. It can be embarrassing if you topple over after coming to a stop and your foot is stuck to the pedal.

Usually you will not be injured by this "accident," but you can hurt yourself falling this way. The injury is minor but your ego gets a big bruise.

Now that you have an introduction to safety equipment, it is time to complete a few sport experiences to get you familiar with the safety equipment (see page 92). Try as many of the experiences as you can.

BICYCLE MAINTENANCE FOR SAFETY

Bicycle maintenance is very important for safety. A poorly maintained bicycle is an accident waiting to happen. Very close attention should be paid to the brakes and wheels. Bad brakes cause many accidents. Double-check the functioning ability of your brakes before each ride. Pop the brake levers several times to make sure that they open and close properly. Check the attaching points of the brakes and the hubs. Anything feeling loose or wobbly should be tightened. Check the wear of your tires and brake pads every week. Refer to Chapter 5 for proper upkeep and maintenance. All you need to know about safety maintenance will be found in that chapter. We regard maintenance as important as safety equipment. If you feel that you cannot properly maintain your bicycle then have someone else do it. Do not neglect maintenance!

BICYCLE SAFETY RULES

Let us now move from safety equipment to safety rules. Rules and practical tips are provided so you will have safe and trouble-free bicycling. It should be noted that most states require bicycles to obey the same traffic laws as motor vehicles. Police issue traffic tickets to bicycles on a regular basis.

1. Always ride with the traffic; never ride into the traffic.
2. Avoid riding on streets where parking is not allowed. Usually the street is too narrow for a car and a bicycle to pass safely.
3. Always obey all traffic regulations, especially stop signs.
4. Always ride single file.
5. Do not ride from in between parked cars.
6. Keep a sharp eye out for car doors opening ahead of you when riding on streets with parked cars.

Do a safety maintenance check on your bicycle. Check the wheels, tires, chain position, and brakes. Make sure that the connections are secure and are functioning properly. Spin the wheels and pedals and check for any improper movement or sounds.

7. Look through the rear window of cars to see if a person is in the position to open a car door in your way.
8. Watch out for young riders; they tend to swerve and do dangerous stunts.
9. Remember pedestrians have the right of way.
10. When riding on sidewalks be very careful of pedestrians.
11. Driveways can be a real hazard; be especially careful if they are partially blocked by shrubs.
12. Keep to the right side of the road.
13. If the road has curbs be careful not to get too close. You can hit the curb with your pedals.
14. Do not carry passengers, except for children in carriers.
15. Keep both hands on the handlebars, especially in traffic.
16. Keep alert for the same potential problems you would if you were driving a car (such as children running out from in between parked cars).
17. As you come to stoplights and stop signs, be alert for cars next to you that want to turn right. They may turn into you.
18. When traffic is heavy, the best way to make a left turn is to cross the street to the other side of the intersection, then walk the bicycle across with the green light.
19. When riding in heavy traffic do not use your toe clips. It is easier to get off your bicycle.
20. Do not ride in unlighted parks at night if police protection is not evident.
21. Keep your brakes in good condition.
22. Keep your tires inflated to proper pressure.
23. Have proper equipment for night riding.

24. Do not speed in heavy traffic.
25. Do not do stunts or zigzag in traffic.
26. Avoid crowded streets.
27. Slow down and look carefully at all intersections.
28. Make all repairs to your bicycle off the road.
29. Dismount and walk across streets if traffic is heavy.
30. Wear special clothing (fluorescent vests) at night.
31. Always check your wheels to make sure axle nuts are tight.
32. Use bicycle paths when they are provided.
33. When possible use less traveled roads and streets.
34. Never ride on freeways (unless posted for riding).
35. Always signal your intentions to turn.
36. Yield the right-of-way to cars and pedestrians.
37. Never hitch rides or ride closely behind any vehicle.
38. Avoid riding a bicycle when you are sick.
39. Avoid riding in rain and snow (brakes do not work well).
40. Practice your riding skills (see Chapter 3).
41. Listen to traffic noise; it can tell you a lot about what is happening around you.
42. Park your bicycle so that it does not interfere with pedestrians.
43. Watch for uneven surfaces and holes when turning (i.e., driveways, large cracks, sewers).
44. Overtake slow-moving trucks and cars on the left; never pass on the right.
45. Do not ride two abreast.

Now that you have read the "rules of the road" it is time to do a few sport experiences that will help you remember the rules (see pages 97–98). Do as many of the experiences as you can.

If you observe the safety rules listed in this chapter, maintain your bicycle, and buy safety equipment, you should have an enjoyable time riding your bicycle. Many riders break the safety rules and cause drivers and pedestrians to hate bicycle riders. We call these people "gorilla" riders. Gorilla riders cause a lot of problems for riders who observe the rules. Many times we wonder why they are still alive considering the stupid stunts they pull in traffic. Don't become a gorilla rider; ride safe and live.

Safety Rules

As you walk or ride in a car observe people who are riding bicycles. As you observe them write down or memorize safety rules you see that are not followed. As you make your list asterisk the broken rules that put the bicyclist in a dangerous situation. Many times safety rules are broken because it is easier to break the rule than to follow the rule (i.e., riding against traffic for one block). Also, write down why you think the rule was broken. Note any bicycling procedures that you think are good safety habits. These would be situations that would be unique to your area.

Bicycle Routes

Pick out the most frequent bike routes you think you will be riding. Walk or drive the routes. As you walk or drive the routes take notes on spots that may be dangerous or potentially dangerous (i.e., crossing a street that is very busy, narrow streets, left turns, etc.). Work out a safety plan that will avoid the trouble spots. You may even have to walk the bicycle for a short distance. Then ride the routes and observe all your plans.

Bicycle Control

These experiences are included to help you gain better control of the bicycle. Good bicycle control leads to a safer ride. These activities can be set up in school parking lots, parking lots after work hours, or areas that have wide sidewalks. It will take you some time to set up the activity but the practice is well worth the effort. You will need old milk cartons or other soft material that if hit will not cause the bicycle to swerve. Place the markers as shown in Figure 4.5. As you get better control move the markers closer together. Also, try to ride through the markers using your mirror. Learn to use your mirror without moving the bicycle from side to side. Then

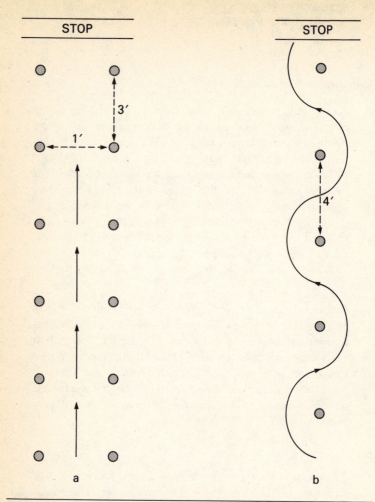

Figure 4.5   Examples of obstacle courses

ride through the markers while turning your head. Note how there is a tendency to move the bicycle toward the side that you have turned your head. Practice until you can control your bicycle without hitting the markers.

WHAT TO DO IF YOU ARE IN AN ACCIDENT

If you are in a car/bicycle accident, first administer first aid and then call the police. Be sure to have the police write up an accident report, including the damage to the bicycle. Get the name and license number of the car driver. Also get the names of all the people who saw the accident. Remember the people in the car that hit you will *not* be witnesses in your favor. You need people outside the car. The biggest problem in bicycle/car accidents is getting the insurance company to pay for your bicycle repairs. That is why it will be necessary for you to go to a bicycle shop and get an estimate of the cost to repair your bicycle. You may have to contact an attorney.

Bicycle Maintenance

There are many different attitudes about maintaining a bicycle in good working order. Some people choose to ignore the maintenance aspect and just ride their bicycle until it quits working. Others will take all maintenance problems to a bicycle shop and completely avoid any up-keep on the bicycle themselves. Some cyclists will do many things with regard to maintenance but will complain about every minute they put into the effort. And still others will look at bicycle maintenance as an enjoyable, relaxing experience. It is really just a matter of attitude on your part. We think that with a little knowledge, practice, and the proper tools, anyone can develop maintenance skills to the point where one can enjoy doing most of the necessary upkeep activities on a bicycle.

Bicycle shops will be happy to take care of all aspects of your bike for a fee; however, you have to remember that they usually have to complete the jobs quickly in order to be cost efficient. We think that in the long run of keeping a bike, the individual owner of a bicycle will take better care of his or her own bike, and of course, at a much better price. Consider this question: "Who cares more about your bike, you or the bike shop?" Obviously, you have more of an investment in your bike than the bike shop. Initially, you may have to sacrifice a little quality with certain skills and you may experience some frustrating moments, but in the long run, it will be worth the trouble. However, if you have lots of money and little time, you may want to take your bike to the same shop for some consistent care.

For many people, the process of taking a bike apart and the feel-ings of satisfaction from completing a task can be a relaxing, enjoyable experience. There is also a feeling of self-confidence and pride from knowing exactly how your bike is put together and how it works. The bike is a relatively simple machine and it can be fun to become a semi-expert on maintenance and upkeep. Try the maintenance activities included in this chapter and see what you think. The activities are arranged from simple to complex. Get comfortable and confident with the simple activities before you attempt the complex ones. Remember that you have to be patient and develop these skills just like your riding skills. The proper tools will also enhance the enjoyment of doing these activities. Do not try to substitute the wrong tools.

MAINTENANCE OF TIRES, TUBES, AND RIMS

Tires need to be replaced as the tread is worn thin. Obviously, the more you ride, the faster your tires will wear out. Be aware that the quality of a tire will enhance the life of the tire. The cheapest is not generally the best deal on a tire. You will usually start to have more and more flat tires as the tread wears thin. This is because the glass, thorns, and nails will be able to work their way through the thin tread easier. You should inspect your tires on a regular basis and when they start to look thin, it is time to change them. In warm climates such as Arizona, some people will have their tires crack from the heat rather than from use. This is another reason to change the tires.

Proper inflation of the tires is an important maintenance point because your bike will ride smoother and handle better. Improperly inflated tires can also cause rim damage. Most cyclists will check the pressure by hand before every ride. Checking the pressure by hand means pushing on the tire with your hand to see if it feels satisfactory. A tire gauge should be used at least once a week. You need to inflate the tire to the stated pressure on the side of the tire. Be sure to use a frame or floor pump that has the proper connection for your tire valve. There are two common types of valves on most bicycle tires: Schrader and Presta valves. It is also important to use a pump rather than a compressed air machine at a service station. The air machine will put air into the tube too quickly and can easily burst a tube. Another problem that can occur is that the bead of the tire can be improperly seated and will not inflate properly. You will see a large bulge in the unseated area. It means that you have to let the air out and work the casing of the tire into the proper position before reinflating.

You are probably aware by now that there are two types of tires and tubes: clinchers and tubulars (see Chapter 2). It is necessary to replace a tire with the same kind of tire. Tubulars are high performance tires that are primarily used by advanced cyclists. Most beginners and intermediate riders will be using clincher tires and tubes, consequently, we will focus our discussion on the clinchers. If you are using tubulars and desire more information on maintenance and upkeep, we suggest that you look at the recommended reading section in Appendix D.

Removing Front Tires and Tubes

Changing the front tire is easiest because you do not have to get your hands greasy from the chain and freewheel. The first thing to do is to let the air out of the tire and open the quick-release lever on the front brake if you have one. This lever will open the brake calipers to allow the tire to come out easily. The next step is to release the hub lever or the nuts that hold the axle to the frame. The quick release lever will simply pull outward from the hub. This is where you will begin to appreciate the quick release equipment. The tire should now come out of the front forks easily. Some people like to turn their bikes upside-down to get the tires out while others will lay the bike on its side. Others will just lift up on the handlebars and pull the tire out and then rest the bike on the front forks.

You are now ready to remove the tire from the rim. You need a set of three bicycle tire irons (see Figure 5.1). These are inserted between

Figure 5.1   Tire irons inserted in a tire

Practice the steps in removing the front wheel, tire, and tube as described. Then reassemble everything in the proper position.

the tire and the rim in order to work the tire off the rim. The rounded flat end of the iron is inserted and the edge of the tire is pried upward until you can hook the notched end of the iron on one of the spokes. Be careful to avoid inserting the tire iron too far because it can cause damage to the tube inside. The second tire iron is inserted about two to four inches away from the first and this procedure is repeated until the tire is off the rim. Another helpful point is to start this process on the side opposite the valve and remove the valve last.

Once you get a portion of the tire bead away from the rim, you can run your fingers around the inside of the tire and slowly pull the rest of the tire away from the rim. Be careful as you run your finger around the inside of the tire because there may be glass slivers or thorns. The tube will now start to come out from inside the tire. At this time, you can inspect the inside of the tire for materials that can cause a flat or have already caused a flat. Be careful because you may find thorns, pieces of glass, nails, or tacks, and these can hurt the fingers. You can also inspect the outside portion of the rim that touches the rim. Usually, there is a large rubber band that goes around the rim. Check to see if there are any sharp points on the spokes that could be causing problems.

Patching Tubes

Now that you have your tube out of the tire, it is time to look for leaks and to patch them up. The best way to find leaks is with a sinkful or panful of water. Just rotate the tube around in the water until you see the air bubbles and you have the leaks located. If you do not have water available, you may be able to hear or feel the air if you pump up the tube enough. Sometimes the valve will be leaking and it will be necessary to tighten the inside core with a metal valve cap. This inside core can also be replaced with a new one.

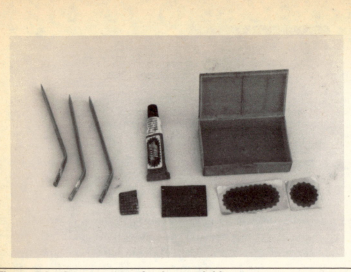

Figure 5.2   Components of a tire patch kit

After the hole has been located, it is a good idea to mark the spot with a yellow crayon or a ballpoint pen because it is easy to lose the spot. It is now time to get out your bicycle patch kit (see Figure 5.2). A small metal grater or piece of sandpaper is provided to rough up the area that will hold the patch. Make sure that the roughed area is wider than the patch and is centered over the hole. If the hole is near the valve, there is a good chance that the patch will not hold and you may have to buy a new tube. After you have roughed the area, you now need to apply a layer of cement to this area. After the cement dries, you can remove the backing from a patch and apply the patch. Keep your fingers away from the area where the patch goes and from the sticky portion of the patch. If you touch the patch or tube, it may not stick well. Fi-

Acquire an old used tube and practice locating the holes. Select a hole and practice the proper procedure for patching. Check the hole for leaks.

Practice cutting an old tube for a protective insert and cement the insert in place.

nally, push the patch on tightly all the way around the perimeter of the patch and hold it tightly for a couple of minutes. Carefully peel the cellophane off the outside of the patch. Test the tube with a low amount of air pressure and if it holds the air, you are ready to mount the tube and tire.

Inserting a Protective Material Inside the Tube

While you have your tire and tube off the rim, it is a good time to install some type of a protective insert between the inside of the tire and the tube. There are commercially made plastic inserts such as one called Mr. Tuffy that costs about five dollars. These will work fine or you can make one yourself with an old thorn-resistant tube. The tube should be cut into a top and bottom half (see Figure 5.3). The bottom half will have the stem attached and this half can be thrown away. The top half of the tube goes next to the inside of the tire tread, not on the sides. It can be glued in place with contact cement. This will reinforce

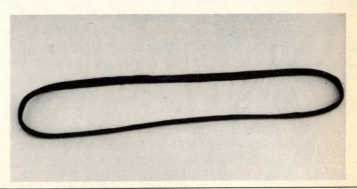

Figure 5.3　An old tube for an insert

Bicycle Maintenance

the tire and protect the tube. This will provide an inexpensive system to prevent punctures from thorns and small nails. You are now ready to put the tube and tire back in place on the rim.

Mounting the Front Tire and Tube

Mounting the tire and the tube can be more difficult than removing them. Start by checking the rubber protective band that goes around the rim. If it looks normal, then place one side or bead of the tire all the way around the rim. The tube goes on next with the valve going into place first in an upright position, not at a slant. Pull the valve into the hole in the rim until it is snug with the rim. There may be a problem with the valve being too wide for the size of the hole in the rim. In that case, you will have to push the valve slightly back into the tube so that the wires on the clincher tires will seat properly. Place the rest of the tube inside the tire all the way around the rim. You are now ready to work the second side or bead of the tire on to the rim. Start at the valve and slowly work the tire into place around the rim. As you get to the last section of the tire, it will become more difficult. Some people will use the tire irons to pop the last section into place. If you can avoid this and still get the tire in place, you are better off because you can avoid damage to your tube with the tire iron.

After you have the tire assembled, place a small amount of air in the tube and check to see if the tire is seated properly in place. You can inspect the tire and rim carefully to see if there are any uneven bulging spots where the tire is not down far enough on the rim. You may have to continue to work and manipulate the tire down until it seats properly. This is especially common with a new tire. It may be necessary to put some air in the tube and then let it out again several times until the casing of the tire is in the correct spot.

The tire and rim are now ready to be put back on the front fork. This involves sliding the tire through the brake calipers and lining up the axle with the front fork ends. The quick release hubs and brake levers should be put back into place by pushing the levers in the direction that tightens them up. The wheel should be aligned so that it spins freely. A hint for tightening the quick release hub is to put the lever in the released position and tighten the opposite side until it is hand tight (tight as you can get it with your hands); then lock the lever back into the tightened position. It is a good idea to line the lever up with the front fork so that it will not stick out and catch on something.

Removing and Mounting the Rear Wheel

The rear wheel is more difficult to remove than the front because of the freewheel and the chain. It is best to put the chain on the small sprockets in the front and the rear. This will make it easier to get the chain off and back on the freewheel. As we mentioned with the front wheel, some cyclists like to put the bike upside down, others put the bike on its side, and still others take the tire out in an upright position. If you have a pannier rack on the back, it is easier to hold on to the rack as you pull the wheel out. You may also want to consider hanging your bicycle from the ceiling with two overhead straps.

It is best to let all the air out of the back tire. Next, the quick release levers on the hub and the brake should be released. If you do not have the release levers, then the retaining nuts on the hubs will have to be loosened with a wrench. The wheel will slide forward slightly out of the dropouts and then down. You will have to lift the top loop of the chain off the freewheel and slide the freewheel down past the derailleur and the lower loop of the chain (see Figure 5.4). It is nice to have a small grease rag for handling the chain at this point. When the wheel is out, do not rest the bike on the derailleur when you put the bike down. Put the bike on its side if you are going to leave it for awhile.

When you are ready to put the wheel back in place, you follow the same procedure by lining up the freewheel inside the chain loop and

Figure 5.4   Rear wheel dropping out past the chain

Figure 5.5   Freewheel removal tool in place

lining up the dropouts with the rear axle. The wheel should go back into place with the chain on the smallest cog on the freewheel. With a little practice, it is a fairly easy procedure to get the rear tire on or off.

If you need to remove the freewheel while you have the rear wheel off, remember that each freewheel brand or make has a special tool that will fit in the freewheel just for the purpose of removing it (see Figure 5.5). A large adjustable wrench can be used with this special freewheel remover. While you have the freewheel off, it is a good time to clean it and soak it in kerosene. After taking it out of the solvent, spray some

Practice removing the rear wheel, tire, and tube. While you have the wheel off, remove the freewheel. Clean and lubricate the freewheel and reassemble the entire wheel.

WD-40 into the inner ring to flush out any dirt and material. Keep spraying the solvent until the freewheel spins smoothly.

Changing the tire or tube on the rear wheel is exactly the same as the front tire or tube. In most cases, the rear tire will wear faster than the front because it carries more weight. You may find that it is necessary to rotate your tires periodically to get better wear on the rear tire. Some people will wear out two rear tires to every one front tire.

Truing the Rims

Truing or straightening a rim is easy to do when you have a little knowledge and patience. The truing process should be done in small steps that should be repeated several times until the wheel is straight. You will need a spoke tightener tool and a black felt-tip type marking pen. The first step is to find a way to support your bike and be able to spin the wheel. Most people prefer to turn the bike upside down but it can be done in an upright position if you have a little help.

The marking pen should be braced against the top of the front or rear brake pad as the wheel is being spun (see Figure 5.6). The brake pad should support the pen so that it will be stable. Slowly move the pen toward the spinning rim until it makes contact with the rim. The pen will mark the rim where it is too far out of line on that side. Now repeat this process on the opposite side and the pen will mark the portions on the other side that are too far out of line. The rim is now marked where it is out of alignment.

The next step is to tighten the spokes that will draw the rim back into proper alignment. A word of caution to beginners: do not turn the spokes more than a half-turn at one time. If you tighten them too tight, you can pull the tire out of round into an elliptical shape. We recommend that you try only a quarter-turn and then retest. The spokes are tightened at the rim by turning the spoke nut clockwise with the spoke tightener. Be sure to use the proper size on the tightener tool that fits your spokes. The black marks on the rim will tell you where to start the tightening process. The spokes that come up from the hub on the opposite side of the rim need to be tightened to draw the rim away from where the rim is hitting the pen. For example, if you are working where the marks are on the left side of the rim, you need to tighten the spokes that come up from the right side of the rim. Do not tighten the spokes that come from the hub on the same side that you are working on because that would only increase the misalignment even more.

This tightening process should continue until you have worked on

Figure 5.6   Position for marking pen in the truing process

all of the areas where the rim is hitting the pen on both sides of the rim. Be sure to remove the pen marks as you work so that you will not duplicate your work on a given area. You should have now removed most of the bent areas. You will have to repeat this process several times depending on the degree of the problem. Remember to be patient and repeat the process several times until the rim is straight. If you practice this process on a regular basis, the problem should be quite small.

THE **SPORT** EXPERIENCE

Practice the truing process as described on your front rim. Then try the process on the back rim. Try the process on a variety of different bicycle styles, i.e., 10-speed, cruiser, BMX.

MAINTENANCE OF CHAINS

The chain is an important part of the bicycle that is easy to maintain without a great deal of skills, yet there are many bikes that have a chain full of dirt and caked-on grease just because of neglect. In addition, many people will use the same chain for years and years because they do not realize that a chain stretches and wears out. A new chain still only costs about five to eight dollars and is simple to replace. In fact, we recommend that you replace your chain about once a year or year and a half. A chain will stretch, loosen up, and wear quite a bit in a year's time. Every month or so the chain should be removed and soaked in kerosene so that it can be cleaned and lubricated. There is a new chain cleaner reservoir made by Vetta available that can be used without removing the chain; however, some people are questioning its effectiveness in cleaning. You just fill the reservoir with solvent, insert the chain, and spin the crank.

Depending on weather conditions, the chain should be wiped clean and lubricated while on the bike about once every other week. There are many different types of oil and grease that can be recommended for a chain. We have had good luck with the following: Bull Shot, Tri-Flow, LPS #3, Silicone Lubricant, and WD-40. It is really a matter of personal preference. If you are new to an area, you should seek the advice of an established bicycle shop owner to see what is recommended for the local weather conditions. There are many conflicting ideas about chain care. Regular care should involve wiping off the excess dirt and oil, spraying on a new coat, and wiping off the excess. Excess lubricant will only collect more dust and dirt. It is a good idea to spray the lubricant with a small plastic tube that is available with the lubricant. This will isolate the lubricant on each link. You can hold a rag under each link to keep the spray from hitting everything else, especially the rims.

Taking off most 10-speed chains requires the use of a device called a chain breaker or chain tool. This tool fits on the chain and is lined up so that it will drive a rivet partly through a chainlink by turning a small handle (see Figure 5.7). The key is to drive out the rivet only far enough to remove the attached link. Do not drive the rivet all of the way out. If you drive the rivet all of the way out of the link, then you will have a big problem getting the rivet back into the chain. Once you have the chain off, you can wind it up in a circle and soak it in a pan of kerosene or similar solvent. General laundry detergent is also effective for soaking and cleaning the chain. Let the chain soak for several

Figure 5.7 Chain tool lined up on the chain

hours and then take it out and let it dry. Make sure that you have all the solvent off before you spray on the new lubricant.

When you are ready to put the chain back into place, line up the chain tool with the rivet and crank the handle until the rivet goes back into the link. At this point, you have to loosen the link by bending the chain back and forth laterally at the exact link. This will prevent a frozen or stiff link which can be a common problem for beginning chain removers. You can also insert a small flathead screwdriver into the link and loosen up the link.

Many chains will have a master link that can be removed with a pair of pliers. The pliers are placed on the two rivets and squeezed together slightly until the special clip will pop off. This link is usually easier to remove and you do not need a special tool. However, the clip on the master link can break and leave you stranded. It is a good idea to carry a spare clip with you or with your tools for changing a flat.

Practice removing the chain with the chain tool. Clean the chain and lubricate properly. Place the chain back on your bicycle.

MAINTENANCE OF PEDALS

As you know from Chapter 2, there are many different types of pedals from the more expensive to disposable throwaways. If you have the inexpensive rubber treaded type, it needs very little maintenance. A few drops of oil or a squirt of lubricant on the axle and a good spin of the pedal are all that it takes. However, these pedals will bend, get out of line, and will wear out much quicker than the more expensive ones that have packed bearings on both ends. After the inexpensive pedals get bent and wobbly, it is time to throw them away and get a new pair. We recommend the better pedals that require a little more maintenance.

With the better pedals, you need to take them apart and repack the bearings with grease about once or twice each year. It is possible to remove the entire pedal from the crank or you can repack the bearings with the pedal attached to the crank. Removing the pedal adds one more thing to do but it allows you to put the pedal on a workbench and eliminate leaning over to work. If you decide to remove the pedals from the cranks, you need a large adjustable wrench because the pedals are usually on pretty tight. It is also necessary to know that the direction you turn the wrench is quite confusing because there is a left pedal and a right pedal. They are not interchangeable. They are usually marked with an R and an L. A good way to remember how to remove the pedals is to put the wrench on the pedal with the wrench sticking straight up. From that position, always loosen to the rear of the bike to remove the pedals. To replace the pedals, always tighten toward the front of the bike.

The first step in dismantling the pedal is to remove the outside cap with an adjustable wrench or a special flat closed-type wrench made by the manufacturer of the pedal. Inside the cap you will find in this order: a lock nut, a washer with a notch that fits in the groove in the axle, a cone-shaped nut that holds the bearings in place, and the bearings which are usually floating freely in some type of grease. It is a good idea to use an egg carton to keep the parts in order as you remove them. We recommend that you remove one pedal at a time so that the parts do not get confused. Be careful as you pull the pedal off the axle because the bearings on the other side of the pedal will come falling out as you remove the pedal.

You now need to clean off all the old grease and repack the bearings in new bicycle grease. There are many types of grease available from your local dealer. Again, check on the type of grease that will work best for the conditions in your area. The bearings on the inside

Practice removing, greasing, and reassembling the pedals of your bicycle and then get permission to dismantle the pedals of bicycles that have different types of pedals.

of the pedal go in first and then the pedal is slid over the axle. The bearings on the other side are placed in next followed by the cone-shaped nut. The notched washer and then the lock nut are last to put in place before the outside cap.

The skill involved requires a snug fit with the cone nut against the bearings. By spinning the pedals you can get the feel of the fit after the cone nut is snug. If you feel that the bearings are grinding together too tightly, then back the cone up a little. If the pedal wobbles from side to side and up and down when you move it manually, the cone is too loose. Once you get the cone nut in the correct position, hold it in place with a wrench or pliers while tightening the lock nut. Be careful to hold the cone nut in place while tightening because it is easy to move and then you have to start adjusting the cone nut all over again. This skill takes a little practice, so be patient while learning. It is easy to get the cone nut too loose or too tight. The correct tools are necessary to keep this job from becoming frustrating. Remember that this proper tightening skill is very similar to working on open hubs and the bottom bracket. You will be able to use the skill many times over and over if you maintain your own bike.

MAINTENANCE OF THE FRONT AND REAR HUBS

Both the front and rear hubs come with either open or sealed bearings. The sealed hubs are relatively new and are more expensive. They will last for long periods of time without any maintenance. However, after a sealed hub fails to function, a new replacement hub must be inserted. This requires special equipment and special skill that a bike shop will have to provide. Each set of sealed bearings is different and it will be necessary to find the exact replacement. We recommend that you ask lots of questions about sealed hubs before you purchase them at your local bike shop. Many people insist that sealed hubs are superior to open hubs. The price of sealed bearings seems to be justified if they last for many years.

The standard open hubs require a repacking of the bearings with grease just like the pedals. It is a very similar process but it does require some time and energy. This repacking process should be done at least once a year. If you ride in the rain and foul weather, you should repack them more often. A set of flat cone wrenches are necessary to hold the cone nut in the correct position while tightening the lock nut (see Figure 5.8). The lock nut should be tightened with an adjustable wrench while the cone wrench is holding the cone nut securely in the proper place. The test for the proper tightness of the bearings is to slowly turn the axle in place. As with the pedals, the cone nut should be snug rather than too tight (a grinding type of feeling) or too loose (a wobbly feeling of moving the axle from side to side or up and down). Refer back to the section on repacking the pedals.

The first step is to remove the wheel and unscrew the quick release bar that goes through the center of the axle. Next, you will find a round dust cover that needs to be pried off with a screwdriver. The lock nut and flat notched washer are tightened against the cone-shaped nut. These hold the bearings in place. Usually, the bearings are free-floating, however, some bearings are held in place with a metal retainer.

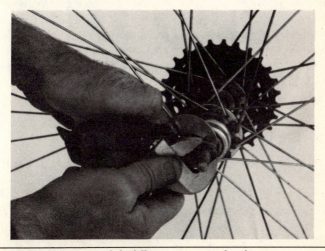

Figure 5.8   Cone wrench holding a cone nut in place

Practice removing the front hub, clean the bearings, regrease, and reassemble.

When you dismantle the hub for the first time, you should assume that the bearings will all fall out when you have everything loose. Be sure to count the bearings so that the correct number is replaced during reassembly. You should replace any of the bearings that are pitted, egg-shaped, have flat spots, or are not shiny when cleaned.

You will find the same arrangement on either side of the axle. Loosen one side and leave the other side as tight as possible. If you loosen both sides, during the reassembling process you will have to adjust both sides to make sure that enough of the axle is sticking out to attach to the front forks. If you have too much axle on one side or the other, then you have a problem. It means that you have to start all over again with your adjusting.

Be sure to be ready to catch the bearings on each side as you slide the axle out from the hub. Most front hubs have ten balls per side and the rear hubs have nine per side. A generous amount of grease should be placed in each of the bearing cup areas. After repacking the bearings with grease, you can begin reassembling the hub by reversing the aforementioned process. The skill that was explained earlier on proper tightening is critical during this process. It is easy to get the bearings too tight or loose and will require some experimentation on the tightness adjustment with the cone wrenches.

The Rear Hub

The rear hub is almost exactly the same as the front except that the freewheel is involved and the axle is a little longer to provide room for the freewheel. The rear hub has a threaded portion where the freewheel attaches. The freewheel should be removed with a freewheel tool as we have explained earlier in this chapter. When you begin to loosen the dust covers and lock nut, etc., it is best to work on the left side of the bike or the side opposite the freewheel. Consequently, you can tighten

Practice removing the rear hub, clean the bearings, regrease, and reassemble.

the right-side cone and lock washer as tight as possible because you do not want them to move again.

After removing the dust cover, lock nut, washer, and cone on the left side, you can now remove the bearings from that side. The axle can then be slid out and the bearings on the right side can be removed. You should clean out all the old grease from inside the hub and off the bearings, nuts, etc. Cones that are pitted or grooved should be replaced. You are now ready to repack the bearings with new grease. Start by packing the grease cup section on the right side and putting the bearings in place. The axle is then slid back into place and the wheel is now turned over. The grease and bearings should now be placed in the left side and the cone nut can be tightened down. This is the critical point for tightening as was explained with the pedals and the front hubs. Go back and review those sections if you are still unclear as to the feel that you should be getting on the tightness of the cone on the bearings. An adjustment that is too tight or too wobbly can cause damage to your hubs. After you have the proper tightness, you are ready to replace the freewheel and put the rim back in place on the frame.

A few words about the rear hub on a standard 3-speed bike are needed in this section. This hub is usually quite complex and is difficult to dismantle. We recommend that you take your 3-speed to a bike shop for rear hub maintenance and ask lots of questions to see if it is in your best interests to dismantle your model. We have not had much success with 3-speed hubs.

MAINTENANCE OF THE BOTTOM BRACKET

Many people are afraid of working on the bottom bracket because the cranks, chainrings, and chain are all in the way. In addition, several specialized tools are needed. We have had good luck with the bottom bracket especially since the cotterless cranks have been developed. We recommend any of the cotterless cranks and think that you should be able to repack the bearings and make adjustments to the bottom bracket with just a little patience, practice, and skill development. Our discussion here will focus on bikes with cotterless cranks. If you do have cranks with cotter pins, you can still do your own work but it is sometimes difficult to get the cotter pins out. Ask your dealer for tips on knocking out the cotter pins. Do not be afraid of all the equipment that you have to remove or the specialized tools that you need. Remember that this is a lifetime commitment and the correct tools will enhance the enjoyment of your maintenance activities. It is also important to understand the incompatibility of equipment for the various brands of bicycles. Many brands are *not* interchangeable, so be sure to buy the tools that fit your bicycle.

We recommend that you first remove the chain and get it out of the way. A good idea is to let it soak in some solvent while you are working on the bottom bracket bearings. Next you want to remove the cranks on both sides. The first step is to remove the plastic or aluminum dust covers with a large flathead screwdriver or an Allen wrench. Remember that the dust cover is not a hard metal and you can gouge or damage it if you use a small screwdriver. The next thing that you will find is a recessed bolt or nut that must be removed with a thin walled socket. This is where you begin to need the first specialized tool called a crankarm bolt spanner (see Figure 5.9). This tool will remove the nut or bolt that holds the crank to the axle. An adjustable wrench is necessary to turn the bolt spanner. Be sure to remove any washers that might be on the axle.

The next step is to use a crank puller to pop the cranks off the axle. The crank puller and bolt spanner are usually connected as one tool. The crank puller portion has two parts involved. The outside ring has threads that screw into the dust cover threads to hold the puller in place. These threads should be tightened as far as possible but only to hand tightness. Make sure that you have backed out the threaded inside rod of the puller to a point where the rod is flush with the inside cup of the puller. This allows you more room for tightening the outside threads into the dust cover threads (see Figure 5.10). If the rod is screwed too far into the inside of the puller, you will not be able to tighten the outside threads enough to secure it properly.

You are now ready to turn the head of the rod until it makes contact with the axle. An adjustable wrench can be used with the flats on the side of the rod. A few turns of the rod and the crank should easily

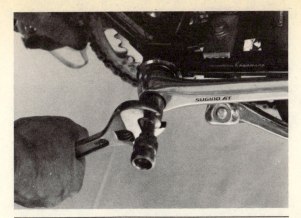

Figure 5.9   Crankarm bolt spanner in place on axle

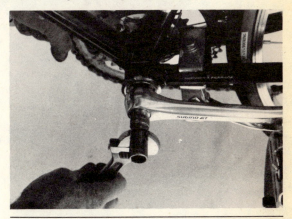

Figure 5.10   Crank puller in place on the crank

pop off the axle. This process should be repeated on the other crank. It is especially important to get the correct puller and spanner for your bike. There are several different sizes, so be sure that you have the correct one. You can do severe damage to your crank threads and axle if you have the wrong size.

Before you begin to dismantle the bearings, etc., you should spin the axle several times to begin getting the feel of the tightness of the bearings. This is similar to the adjustment of the pedal and hub bearings described earlier. The bearings should not bind and the axle should not wobble too much. Somewhere in between these two points

Figure 5.11 C-wrench in place

Figure 5.12 Fixed cup remover in place

is the proper adjustment. The adjustment may take several trials when you put the bearings back together, but this is normal.

After the cranks are removed, the first step to dismantling is to loosen the lockring on the left side of the bike (see Figure 5.11). This requires a special tool called a C-wrench or C-spanner. This tool is also important for making the final tightening adjustments, so be sure to get this tool and do not try knocking the ring loose with a screwdriver and a hammer. After the lockrings come the adjustable bearing cup with the bearings inside the cup. The bearings are usually inside a metal retainer that holds them in place. Covering the middle of the axle is a plastic protective sleeve. On the right side of the bottom bracket is a fixed bearing cup that can be removed with another special tool (see Figure 5.12) that is usually on the opposite end of the C-wrench. The fixed cup can either be left in place or removed. Most people leave it in place because the bearings on that side can be removed from the left side.

It is now time to clean everything and repack the bearings. A light viscosity grease made for bicycle bearings is best. Put plenty of grease in both cups and around the balls in the retainer. The back of the wider side of the bearing retainer should be lightly greased where it will make contact with bearing races or notches on the axle. The narrower side of the bearing retainer goes against the fixed cup, and then the long end of the axle should be slid into position. The long end of the axle always goes on the chainrings side. The plastic cover goes on next and is followed by the adjustable cup with the regreased bearings inserted properly. Many people like to put a business card with their name and address in the plastic sleeve during reassembly because it can be excellent proof of ownership. The lockring is the last piece. Now is the time to test your adjusting skill. A pin spanner or cone wrench will hold the adjustable cup in place while you tighten the lockring with the C-wrench (see Figure 5.13). As you turn the C-wrench, you may get some movement of the adjustable cup and this will alter your tightness adjustment. This is why you have to set your adjustable cone first and try to keep it in the same position while tightening the lockring. Remember that it may take several trials before it is positioned properly.

It is now time to replace the cranks on the axle. Put the right side on first and give it a blow from a rubber mallet to seat it in position. Be

Figure 5.13   Cone wrench and C-wrench in place

Practice the described work on your bottom bracket. Allow yourself plenty of time and patience.

sure to place an immovable object on the opposite side and protect the side you are hammering with a piece of wood or rubber. Lightly grease the treads of the axle and tighten the nut or bolt with the bolt spanner until it is snug. Install the left crank and then give it a spin to see how smoothly it runs. Do not forget the dust covers before replacing the chain. Check the bracket carefully during the next few rides to see if anything is working loose.

HEADSET MAINTENANCE

The headset supports the front fork in the frame with two sets of bearings: one just below the handlebar stem and one just above the front fork. The headset prevents any wobbly motion of the fork and also allows the front fork to rotate in conjunction with the steering of the bike. It is probably the most neglected portion of the bike. Most people ignore the headset unless the steering column becomes frozen or too loose. A conventional headset needs to be cleaned, repacked with grease, and adjusted about once a year. There are sealed headsets that require no maintenance, but once they stop working, you will need a new headset. We recommend a conventional one that can be serviced and components that can be replaced.

The first step is to remove the handlebars and stem by loosening the bolt that holds the stem in place. The locknut on the top of the headset should also be loosened with a headset spanner or a large adjustable wrench. Avoid using a pair of channel locks or vise grips because they will chew up the metal. The bolt on top of the stem should be loosened slightly and then hit with a hammer to dislodge the expander wedge in the stem. A little bit of penetrating oil is helpful at this time. If it does not break free, loosen the bolt a few more turns and hit it again. Be sure to protect the bolt with a block of wood or piece of rubber. You may find that your shift levers are also in the way and they may have to be loosened and slid up out of the way. Next, you will probably find a notched washer and then another threaded adjusting ring that will require a C-wrench similar to the bottom bracket wrench or to some other type of spanner. You may also find a bracket that holds your center pull brakes or a light. Eventually, you will get to a final adjusting ring and the bearings. It is now time to loosen the final ring and take the bearings out and remove the front wheel.

The bike should be turned over at this point to slide the fork out and to remove the bottom bearings. Always assume that the bearings will be loose and will come showering out. In reality, most bearings are in a retainer. You should now be ready to clean everything up and repack the bearings with new grease. The headset goes back together in reverse order. The bottom bearings are repacked first and then the fork is slid back in place. Make sure that the narrow or open side of the bearings retainer is facing the ground when the bike is upside down. The bike should now be turned back to an upright position and the top bearings are repacked. In the upright position, the narrow or open side of the top bearings retainer should also face down.

Lightly grease the steering column threads and start to reassemble with the bottom adjusting ring. Make sure that you do not overtighten the adjusting ring but do not allow it to be so loose that the front fork wobbles. Refer to the section on tightening pedals, hubs, and the bottom bracket. When it is correctly adjusted, slide the lock washer in place and tighten the locknut against the washer and any other brackets, etc., that might be on the column. You can now put your handlebar stem in place and tighten the stem bolt as well as tightening the top locknut. If you have it too tight or loose, you will have to reset the adjustment ring. It may take several trials to get it just right. During the

You are ready to practice dismantling and regreasing the headset on your bicycle. Remember that this is one of the most difficult maintenance procedures.

first few rides, make sure that the headset moves smoothly and the forks are not too loose. Also, be sure to see if the brakes work properly. Check for any loosening of the adjusting rings during the next few weeks.

MAINTENANCE OF THE BRAKES

The brakes are the most important safety component on your bicycle. If you neglect them and allow one or both of them to become non-functional, you will have to slow down and you may also end up flipping the bike over. There is not a lot of regular maintenance on a set of brakes that have been set up properly. Even so, the brakes should be checked regularly. Your bicycle should have a proper set-up in regard to the friction of the brake cables, the length of the brake cables, the brake reach, the position and attachment of the brake levers, and the adjustment of the brake calipers and shoes. As you can see, the set-up and functioning of the brakes involves a great deal of complex information that is beyond the scope of this book. We recommend that you look into the suggested readings at the end of the book for in-depth information on brake set and repair.

From a beginner's perspective, a new or used bike should be checked carefully to see if the brakes are set up and functioning properly. If you cannot get a knowledgeable person to help you, then check to see if the brakes are opening and closing adequately. Try the brakes while the bike is both moving and stationary. The brakes should open and close smoothly. They should not grab or require a push on the levers to open properly. If they do not open and close properly, there may be some minor problems with the calipers or some major problems with the cables and their set-up. If they are not working properly, you should ask a number of questions at this point.

In addition, check to see if the brakes are centered properly over the wheel. They tend to drift to one side and begin to rub on that side of the rim. It may be possible to center the brake by tapping the spring behind the caliper with a screwdriver and a hammer. Squeaking brakes is another problem that can be corrected by slightly toeing in the front of the brake pads. The calipers can be bent in slightly in order to toe in the pad. Do not bend the calipers too much because you can do damage to the brake and bend it too far inward.

As far as general brake maintenance goes, it is a good idea to keep the brakes clean and to spray some lubricant such as WD-40 into all the moving parts and pivot areas about once a month. The pads can easily be replaced when they become worn-looking. However, the brakes will usually function fine for a long time even when the pads start to look worn. Regularly check the nuts that hold the calipers in place. They tend to loosen up and can cause trouble. They need to be tight enough to hold the brake in place but loose enough to allow the brake to function.

MAINTENANCE OF THE GEARS AND THE DRIVE TRAIN

The drive train involves the chain, the freewheel, the front chainrings, the front derailleur, and the rear derailleur. All of these should be kept clean and lubricated so that they function properly. Refer back to the section on chains and freewheels (p. 111) for the discussion on those components. The chainrings simply need to be cleaned regularly with a solvent that will dislodge all the dust, grease, etc. The front and rear derailleurs need to be cleaned and lubricated regularly. The moving parts that pivot, bend, and slide should be sprayed with a lubricant such as WD-40. The many various types of derailleurs have different areas that need to be sprayed. Carefully spray the pivot areas and in the middle of the wheels where the chain rides. There are two areas that are spring loaded. These should be cleaned and sprayed thoroughly. Turn your bike on the side and spray the insides of the small wheels where the the chain rides. Basically, you want to lubricate any part of the derailleurs that are moving parts.

There are several fine adjustments that can be made on the different types of derailleurs. These adjustments can include the derailleur cables, the range of motion screws, and the resting angle of the rear derailleur. These can be simple or quite complex problems. We recommend that you get advice from an advanced biker or a bike shop before you attempt to make these types of adjustments.

MAINTENANCE TOOLS

The key points for bicycle tools are to buy quality tools and the correct tools for your particular bike. If you buy cheap tools, they can chew up the nuts, bolts, and various parts that you are working on. Obviously, you should avoid this situation by adding quality tools as you need

Bicycle Maintenance Checklist

If you are a beginner at bicycle maintenance, this checklist may help you to keep track of the specific areas and the key points of maintenance.

1. Tires
    Adequate tread—changes with wear
    Mounted on the rim properly—no bulges on the side
    Valve stem is straight up
    Proper amount of air
2. Wheels
    Secured properly to front fork
    Rims are clean
    Spokes are tight and wheels are trued
    Centered properly with brakes and frame
3. Headset and Handlebars
    Clean at the top and bottom
    No looseness or wobbling
    Full range of motion for steering
    Not too tight with a grinding feeling during turns
    Repack the bearings once a year
    Handlebars tight and straight
    Replace handlebar tape or covers as needed
    Plugs secure in the handlebar ends
4. Hubs and Bottom Bracket
    Clean exterior
    Spin properly—not too tight or loose
    Repack the bearings once or twice a year
    Clean and lubricate the freewheel twice a month
    Clean the chainrings twice a month
    Check the tightness of the bolts holding the cranks in place
5. Chain
    Clean and lubricate twice a month

Remove and soak in a solvent every other month
Check for wear—loose or stiff links
Replace the chain about once a year
Check the amount of play in the chain—about one inch

6. Pedals
   Clean regularly
   Repack the bearings once or twice a year
   Check for proper attachment
   Check for proper spin—not too tight or loose
   Check the toe straps and replace once a year

7. Brakes
   Cleaned regularly
   Attached and centered properly
   Cables adjusted—not rusted or frayed
   Replace the cables and regrease as needed
   Pads not worn too thin
   Quick release levers working properly
   Levers attached properly
   Lubricate pivot points as needed
   Opening and closing properly
   Adequate braking power

8. Derailleurs
   Clean and lubricate once a month
   Check the pivot points and chain wheels for smoothness
   Chain is shifting smoothly
   Range of motion for the chain is adequate
   Attached properly
   Cables adjusted—not rusted or frayed

9. Saddle
   Secured tightly to the post—no movement
   Height and tilt adjustment should be checked
   Check the wear of the saddle and replace as needed

10. Racks and Accessories
    Check for proper tightness
    Check for proper alignment or position

Maintenance Tools and Equipment Checklist

1. Adjustable crescent wrenches—one small and one large _____
2. Screwdrivers—one small and one large _____
3. Pliers—regular and needlenosed _____
4. Set of metal tire irons _____
5. Hex or Allen wrenches that fit your bike _____
6. Set of cone wrenches that fit your bike for hub adjustment _____
7. A crank spanner and puller for removing the cranks _____
8. A C-spanner wrench and holder wrench (if necessary) for the bottom bracket _____
9. A chain breaker _____
10. A freewheel remover—specifically for your freewheel _____
11. A spoke wrench _____
12. A tube patch kit _____
13. Spray lubricant such as WD-40 or equivalent _____
14. Spray oil for the chain such as Tri-Flow _____
15. Bicycle bearing grease such as Bull Shot _____
16. A can of kerosene or equivalent type solvent _____
17. An old paintbrush and toothbrush for cleaning _____
18. A hand pump or a frame pump _____
19. A pair of channel locks and a vise-grip _____
20. A small knife _____
21. A hammer _____
22. A set of small open-ended wrenches _____

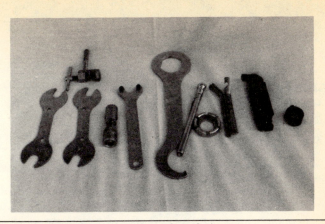

Figure 5.14   Maintenance tools and equipment

them. Remember that these are a lifetime investment and good tools will last that long. It is important to remember that certain tools will only fit certain bikes. If you are uncertain, ask before you buy something that will not fit your bike. We recommend the tools and equipment listed in the checklist on page 128 (see Figure 5.14).

Maintaining your bicycle can be an enjoyable, relaxing activity. Much satisfaction can be gained by dismantling and reassembling the various components of the bicycle. You will also know that everything has been completed correctly if you do it yourself. Proper maintenance of your bicycle will give you a feel of safety and may eliminate an accident that could be caused by a bicycle in need of maintenance.

Going Beyond:
Possibilities for the Future

After you have developed your basic cycling skills, you may wish to extend the use of your bicycle into other areas and activities. The bicycle can be used for many reasons. For example, the bicycle is an excellent way to improve the cardiovascular system. The bicycle is also an excellent way to see the world, and enjoy the great outdoors. Touring on a bicycle is relaxing and an enjoyable type of activity. Building your own bicycle is also very rewarding if you like to work with your hands. This chapter will focus on various special interest activities involving you and your bicycle.

USING THE BICYCLE FOR CARDIOVASCULAR FITNESS

If properly used, the bicycle is an excellent way to attain cardiovascular fitness and muscular endurance. Other forms of activities used by individuals to attain this type of fitness are running and swimming. Running is hard on the legs and hips, while bicycling is easy on the legs. Your legs are subjected to forces up to five times your body weight when running. Bicycling does not produce nearly the forces generated by running since the body weight is supported by the bicycle. Swimming is easy on the legs, but swimming pools are not always easy to find and you can only swim in the warm months (unless you can locate an indoor pool). Roads are always available and most states clear the roads when snow hits. You can ride in inclement weather with the proper

Complete the following worksheet to calculate your target heart rate. An example is under each rule.

To Do

a. Write your age

_____

40

b. Find estimated maximum heart rate. Subtract your age from 220

_____

220 − 40 = 180

c. Sit down for ten minutes and then take your resting heart rate.

_____

65

d. Find range of heart rate, subtract c from b

_____

180 − 65 = 115

e. Take 60 percent of the range. (.60 times d)

_____

.60 × 115 = 69

f. Add 60 percent of the range (from 3) to the resting heart rate (e + c)

_____

69 + 65 = 134

Example: Target Heart Rate = 134 (found in Step f)

clothing. You can also use a stationary bicycle in extremely bad weather.

To use the bicycle for a cardiovascular workout you must first calculate your target heart rate. Target rate is the minimum number of beats per minute your heart should beat to improve or attain cardiovascular fitness.

Postexercise Heart Rate Chart

The following is an example of the way you can record your postexercise heart rate. There is also a copy of the heart rate chart in Appendix A.

Date	____	____	____	____	____
Rate immediately after stopping	____	____	____	____	____
Rate after one minute	____	____	____	____	____
Rate after two minutes	____	____	____	____	____
Rate after three minutes	____	____	____	____	____
Rate after four minutes	____	____	____	____	____
Rate after five minutes	____	____	____	____	____

Use the chart in Appendix A and start charting your postexercise heart rate.

THE *SPORT* EXPERIENCE

The following is a beginning workout program you may wish to try. Appendix A has an intermediate and an advanced workout program. Each program is a progressive program that increases the amount of exercise each week. Feel free to change the programs; they are only suggested formats. In addition, feel free to start anywhere in the program you wish. If the workout is too difficult then drop down to a lighter workout. Remember to always stretch before any workout, and stretch after the workout. If you have muscle soreness 24 hours after the workout, the workout was too difficult. Also note that you can use a stationary bicycle to do most of the workouts, if you are experiencing poor weather.

6-Week Beginning Program

Week 1
Ride 3 days for 10 minutes at target heart rate, rest at least one day between rides. (3 × week for 10 min. @ T.H.R.)

Week 2
Ride 3 days for 15 minutes at target heart rate, rest at least one day between rides. (3 × week for 15 min. @ T.H.R.)

Week 3
Ride 3 days for 20 minutes at target heart rate, rest at least one day between rides. (3 × week for 20 min. @ T.H.R.)

Week 4
Ride 3 days for 25 minutes at target heart rate, rest at least one day between rides. (3 × week for 25 min. @ T.H.R.)

Week 5
Ride 3 days for 30 minutes at target heart rate, rest at least one day between rides. (3 × week for 30 min. @ T.H.R.)

Week 6
Ride 3 days for 35 minutes at target heart rate, rest at least one day between rides. (3 × week for 35 min. @ T.H.R.)

Try the beginning, intermediate, or advanced workout programs we have designed for you.

You should recalculate your target heart rate every six weeks. As you attain better physical conditioning the target heart rate will change. You need to learn to monitor your heart rate while riding your bicycle. To monitor your heart rate you will need a watch with a second hand or a stopwatch. As you ride feel your carotid artery (the big artery in your neck) and take the rate for 10 seconds. Then multiply the number by six. For example if the 10 second rate was 24, the minute rate would be 24 times 6 which equals 144 beats per minute. If your target rate was 134, this would be a little too high. If the 10 second rate was 22, the minute heart rate would be 22 times 6 which equals 132 beats per minute. What most people do is divide their target heart rate by 6, and then try to reach that rate for the 10 second count (i.e., 134 divided by 6 equals 22.3 or approximately 22). In our example, the rider would try to maintain the 10 second rate between 22 and 23 beats. You should take your heart rate about every three minutes during your rides for the first 10 minutes. After the first 10 minutes you only need to take your heart rate every 5 to 10 minutes. If you are so inclined you can buy a heart rate monitor that will give you heart rates instantly during the ride.

After each ride, monitor your heart rate minute by minute for five minutes after you stop. Record your readings. Be sure to take your heart rate immediately after you stop; within 5–10 seconds after you stop.

As you get into better cardiovascular condition, you will find that your heart rate will decrease more rapidly after your workouts. This is a good sign that you are indeed improving your cardiovascular system. As you attain better cardiovascular conditioning, the quicker your heart rate will return to your resting rate after exercise. When you are in excellent cardiovascular condition you will see a large decrease in your heart rate during the first minute after exercise (i.e., 134 beats to 75 beats in the first minute).

TOURING WITH YOUR BICYCLE

Touring with a bicycle can be a lot of fun, and it is an interesting way to see our country or other places in the world. Many people see part of Europe by bicycle. Bicycle touring involves riding from place to place (distance will vary with the individual or group) during the day and staying overnight at campgrounds or hotels. Most people pack their needed gear on the bicycle and buy food along the way. If you want, you can even find groups that tour in the snow (they use all-terrain bicy-

Figure 6.1   Pannier placement—high rear and low front

cles). If you think you would like to tour with a bicycle, you must determine if your present bicycle can be converted into a touring bicycle. Most derailleur bicycles can be converted into touring bicycles.

The most important thing to check on your bicycle is your current bicycle's chainstay length. If the length of the chainstay is 17 or more inches long you can convert your bicycle to a touring bicycle. The chainstay length needs to be longer than 16 inches for the attachment of the panniers to the rear of the bicycle. If the chainstay length is too short then your heels will not clear the panniers when you pedal. You should also invest in a new set of rims and tires. Good touring rims have 40 or more spokes and touring tires are heavier than normal tires. You will find the bumps are not as hard with the larger tires and rims. It would also be wise to use 14-gauge spokes in the wheels (most good touring rims have 14-gauge spokes). The extra strong spoke is needed to help support the extra weight you will carry in the panniers and on the bicycle (40 or more pounds).

Of course you will have to buy panniers for your bicycle, to hold all your touring gear. There are several combinations of front, rear, and handlebar panniers. Placement of the panniers is important. Research has proven that the best combination of panniers is to have a high rear pannier, a low front pannier, and a small handlebar pannier (see Figure 6.1 for correct placement of panniers). This combination had the best results for handling the bicycle. Never have a large handlebar pannier;

you will not have good control of your bicycle at higher speeds. Research has also shown that the weight should be distributed between the front and rear panniers.

You may wish to change your gearing for touring. You will need lower gears to climb hills and to pull the extra weight. Many people also add a third chainring (called a granny gear) to the crank (see Figure 6.2). This small chainring can be a real lifesaver when climbing long hills with a large load on your bicycle.

Training for touring is open to disagreement. Some experts state that there is no way to train for day-after-day cycling with 40 or more pounds on the bicycle. They feel that on long tours the best training is the trip itself. We tend to disagree with that attitude. If you train four days a week, doing 30 to 40 miles per day with weight on your bicycle, we feel you will be ready for touring. Be sure to include hills in your workouts. If you do the workouts in this chapter and then do the weight bearing workouts for three weeks before the tour, you will be ready!

If you have never toured before it is best to start with a tour group. Most groups will have a sag wagon (a van or bus that carries extra parts and even some luggage, and once in a while a tired bicyclist). Pick your group with care. Make sure that the others on the tour are your type of people. Nothing could be worse than to end up with a group of people you have nothing in common with, and do not care to be around. After you have a few tours under your belt, you may wish to plan your own tour. Planning your own tour can be lots of fun. You can tour by yourself or with a person that fits your conditioning and general bicycling abil-

Figure 6.2   Granny gear on chainring

Find out about your local touring club. Obtain information about the types of trips the club takes and if it is the type of club you would wish to join.

ity. There are several good books on the market to help you with your tour planning. We suggest that you buy some of these books and read them before you venture out on your own (see the recommended readings in Appendix D).

BUILDING YOUR OWN BICYCLE

Building your own bicycle can be fun and challenging. For those people who like a real challenge, frame building is an interesting project. However, most people do not make their own frames. In reality, building your own bicycle means putting the components on a bicycle frame; very few people can make the components needed to build a bicycle. If you buy all the components to put together a bicycle, you will pay two to three times what it would cost to buy a complete bicycle at the bicycle store. What you will need to do is to find good components at a reasonable cost. Part of the challenge in building your own bicycle is to build it for a reasonable cost.

To put together your own bicycle you must first start with a frame. You can buy frames at most bicycle stores. You will pay a lot for a good frame. However, the frame is the most important part of the bicycle. You can find excellent frames at police and other bicycle auctions. Many times bicycles at auctions have been stripped and about all that is left is the frame, fork, and crank. Bicycle thieves will take the wheels, gears, or seat but will leave the crank and handlebars and fork. Go to the auction and look the bicycles over. Review the section in Chapter 2 on frames so you will know a good frame when you find one. You will be surprised at the quality of frames at a police auction. Be sure to check the frame carefully to make sure it is not bent. While at

Look for bicycle frames and components in the want ads of your local newspaper. You can pick up some excellent buys from the want ads. Check your local bicycle clubs; many times you can get good deals on components from members in the club.

the auction, also look for components that you can use. A word of caution: try to find common brand-name frames; it may be hard to find components that fit off-brand frames.

You may also want to try to build your own wheels. You might find good rims but they will need new spokes. Go ahead and put new spokes in the hub and rim yourself (called lacing), but let the bicycle store true the wheel for roundness. The big problem in doing your own wheels is getting the hub in the exact center of the wheel. The bicycle shop has special equipment to center the hub.

OFF-ROAD RECREATION ACTIVITIES

There is a growing number of people who take to the wilderness with their bicycles. These people use the all-terrain bicycle that is built for off-road riding. This is a great way to enjoy the outdoors. The all-terrain bicycle is quiet and does much less damage to the earth than an all-terrain vehicle. There are tours for off-road bicycles, just as there are tours for the dropped handlebar derailleur bicycle. If you are interested in all-terrain touring we suggest that you pick up a copy of a bicycling magazine. You will find information on tours and equipment in these magazines.

The all-terrain bicycle group has formed the National Off-Road Bicycle Association. They have published a set of codes for off-road bicyclists to follow. If the code is followed, off-road touring and racing will be an acceptable form of recreation (see Figure 6.3).

Now that you have read this book and participated in the sport ex-

Figure 6.3 Off-road exploring

periences, you should be ready to enter the exciting world of cycling! You should be able to enjoy all the activities that are possible with a bicycle. We will see you on the road!

Using Your Bicycle for Cardiovascular Fitness

Postexercise Heart Rate Chart

Date ____ ____ ____ ____ ____

Rate immediately
after stopping ____ ____ ____ ____ ____

Rate after one
minute ____ ____ ____ ____ ____

Rate after two
minutes ____ ____ ____ ____ ____

Rate after three
minutes ____ ____ ____ ____ ____

Rate after four
minutes ____ ____ ____ ____ ____

Rate after five
minutes ____ ____ ____ ____ ____

Date ____ ____ ____ ____ ____

Rate immediately
after stopping ____ ____ ____ ____ ____

Rate after one
minute ____ ____ ____ ____ ____

Rate after two
minutes ____ ____ ____ ____ ____

Rate after three
minutes ____ ____ ____ ____ ____

Rate after four
minutes ____ ____ ____ ____ ____

Rate after five
minutes ____ ____ ____ ____ ____

Date	____	____	____	____	____
Rate immediately after stopping	____	____	____	____	____
Rate after one minute	____	____	____	____	____
Rate after two minutes	____	____	____	____	____
Rate after three minutes	____	____	____	____	____
Rate after four minutes	____	____	____	____	____
Rate after five minutes	____	____	____	____	____

6-Week Intermediate Program

Week 1

Ride 4 days for 35 minutes at target heart rate, rest one day between rides (4 × week for 35 min. @ T.H.R.).

Week 2

Ride 4 days for 40 minutes at target heart rate, rest one day between rides (4 × week for 40 min. @ T.H.R.).

Week 3

Ride 4 days for 45 minutes at target heart rate, rest one day between rides (4 × week for 45 min. @ T.H.R.).

Week 4

Ride 4 days for 50 minutes at target heart rate, rest one day between rides (4 × week for 50 min. @ T.H.R.).

Week 5

Ride 4 days for 55 minutes at target heart rate, rest one day between rides (4 × week for 55 min. @ T.H.R.).

Week 6

Ride 4 days for 60 minutes at target heart rate, rest one day between rides (4 × week for 60 min. @ T.H.R.).

6-Week Advanced Program

Week 1

Day 1	60 minute ride at target heart rate (60 min. @ T.H.R.).
Day 2	Hill work: do 10 repeats up a quarter-mile hill (10 × hills).
Day 3	Rest
Day 4	60 minute ride at target heart rate (60 min. @ T.H.R.).
Day 5	10 quarter-mile sprints at top speed, rest between sprints until heart rate is down to 120.
Day 6	Rest
Day 7	60 minute ride at target heart rate (60 min. @ T.H.R.).

Week 2

Day 1	65 minute ride at target heart rate (65 min. @ T.H.R.).
Day 2	Hill work: do 12 repeats up a quarter-mile hill (12 × hills).
Day 3	Rest
Day 4	65 minute ride at target heart rate (65 min. @ T.H.R.).
Day 5	12 quarter-mile sprints at top speed, rest between sprints until heart rate is down to 120.
Day 6	Rest
Day 7	65 minute ride at target heart rate (65 min. @ T.H.R.).

Week 3

Day 1	65 minute ride at target heart rate (65 min. @ T.H.R.).
Day 2	Hill work: do 15 repeats up a quarter-mile hill (15 × hills).
Day 3	Rest
Day 4	65 minute ride at target heart rate (65 min. @ T.H.R.).
Day 5	15 quarter-mile sprints at top speed, rest between sprints until heart rate is down to 120.
Day 6	Rest
Day 7	65 minute ride at target heart rate (65 min. @ T.H.R.).

Week 4

Day 1	65 minute ride at target heart rate (65 min. @ T.H.R.).
Day 2	Hill work: do 18 repeats up a quarter-mile hill (18 × hills).
Day 3	Rest
Day 4	65 minute ride at target heart rate (65 min. @ T.H.R.).
Day 5	18 quarter-mile sprints at top speed, rest between sprints until heart rate is down to 120.
Day 6	Rest
Day 7	65 minute ride at target heart rate (65 min. @ T.H.R.).

Week 5

Day 1	3 or 4 hour ride at good pace. Heart rate at 120 or better.
Day 2	Rest
Day 3	Hill work: do 18 repeats up a quarter-mile hill (18 × hills).
Day 4	65 minute ride at target heart rate (65 min. @ T.H.R.).
Day 5	18 quarter-mile sprints at top speed, rest between sprints until heart rate is down to 120.
Day 6	Rest
Day 7	65 minute ride at target heart rate (65 min. @ T.H.R.).

Week 6

Day 1	3 or 4 hour ride at good pace. Heart rate at 120 or better.
Day 2	Rest
Day 3	Hill work: do 18 repeats up a quarter-mile hill (18 × hills).
Day 4	65 minute ride at target heart rate (65 min. @ T.H.R.).
Day 5	18 quarter-mile sprints at top speed, rest between sprints until heart rate is down to 120.
Day 6	Rest
Day 7	65 minute ride at target heart rate (65 min. @ T.H.R.).

Appendix B
Gearing Chart

Gearing charts are based on the English unit system. Gearing charts show the size a wheel would be if it were to move an equivalent distance with one pedal revolution. Since we do not buy different size wheels, the gearing ratio will tell you if it is a hard gear or easy gear. Gears in the 90 and above range are very hard and take a large amount of strength to turn the wheels. 70 to 90 gear range are used by most bicyclists; good riders can use the low end of this range to climb hills. 50 to 70 gear range is used by most noncompetitive riders to climb hills; 35 to 50 gear range will be used if the bicycle is loaded and climbing a long hill.

The formula for computing the gear ratio is as follows:

$$\text{ratio} = \frac{\text{number of teeth on chainring}}{\text{number of teeth on cog}} \times \text{ wheel diameter}$$

For example: 27-inch wheel, a chainring with 40 teeth, and a cog with 17 teeth ($40/17 \times 27 = 63.5$).

You will need to make a decision concerning the gears you will want on your bicycle. Use the above formula to compute the gears.

Appendix C
Bicycle Clubs and Organizations

Amateur Bicycle League
   of America
4233 205th Street
Bayside, Long Island, NY 11361

American Youth Hostels
National Campus
Delaplane, VA 22025

Bikecentennial
P.O. Box 8308
Missoula, MT 59807

British Cycling
   Federation
26 Par Crescent
London W1 England

Canadian Cycling
   Association
333 River Rd.
Vanier, Ontario, Canada K11 8B9

Canadian Youth Hostels
   Association
268 First Avenue
Ottawa, Ontario, Canada

League of American Wheelmen
P.O. Box 988
Baltimore, MD 21203

The Bicycle Touring Group
3509 Grove Avenue
Suite 3-E
Richmond, VA 23221

The International Bicycle Touring
   Society
2115 Paseo Dorado
La Jolla, CA 92037

United States Cycling Federation
1750 East Boulder
Colorado Springs, CO 80909

Vermont Bicycle Touring
R.D. 2B
Bristol, VT 05443

Appendix D
Resources

Books

Brandt, J. *The Bicycle Wheel.* Menlo Park, CA: Avocet Inc., 1981.

Coles, C. W., and H. T. Glenn. *Glenn's Complete Bicycle Manual.* New York: Crown Publishers, Inc., 1973.

Doughty, T., E. Pavelka, and B. George. *The Complete Book of Long Distance and Competitive Cycling.* New York: Simon and Schuster, 1983.

Durry, J., and J. B. Wadley. *Bicycling: A Guinness Superlatives Guide.* New York: Sterling Publishing Co., 1977.

Fichter, G. S., and K. Kingbay. *Bicycling.* Racine, Wisconsin: Western Publishing Co., 1974.

Forester, John. *Effective Cycling.* Cambridge, MA: MIT Press, 1984.

Hoyt, Creig S., and Julie Hoyt. *Cycling.* Dubuque, Iowa: Wm. C. Brown Company, 1978.

Teresi, Dick, and Doug Colligan. *The Cyclist's Manual.* New York: Sterling Publishing Co., 1982.

Walton, Bill, and Bjarne Rostaing. *Bill Walton's Total Book of Bicycling.* New York: Bantam Books, 1985.

Wolf, Ray (ed.). *Bicycling Magazine's All Terrain Bikes.* Emmaus, PA: Rodale Press, 1985.

Wolf, Ray (ed.). *Bicycling Magazine's Bicycle Repair.* Emmaus, PA: Rodale Press, 1985.

Wolf, Ray (ed.). *Bicycling Magazine's Bicycle Touring.* Emmaus, PA: Rodale Press, 1985.

Wolf, Ray (ed.). *Bicycling Magazine's Easy Bicycle Maintenance.* Emmaus, PA: Rodale Press, 1985.

Wolf, Ray (ed.). *Bicycling Magazine's Fitness Through Cycling.* Emmaus, PA: Rodale Press, 1985.

Wolf, Ray (ed.). *Bicycling Magazine's Riding and Racing Techniques.* Emmaus, PA: Rodale Press, 1985.

Magazines

Bicycling, Rodale Press Inc., 33 E. Minor Rd., Emmaus, PA 18049.
BMX Action, 3162 Kashiwa St., Torrance, CA 90505.
Velo-News: A Journal of Bicycle Racing, 67 Main St., Box 1257, Brattleboro, VT 05301.
Winning, Bicycle Racing Illustrated, Inc., 1127 Hamilton St., Allentown, PA 18101.

Index

Make cycling a sport for life. Here's an activity that can enhance both your physical and psychological well-being while giving you hours of fun with friends and competitors.

Master teachers Paul Darst and Lee Burkett give you all the information and time-tested tips you need—from selecting the best bicycle for you to handling all aspects of bicycle maintenance—plus contagious enthusiasm for a sport well performed.

You'll learn how to incorporate cycling into your lifestyle aided by activities called The Sport Experience, and when you need help with your cycling skill, The Error Corrector, found in appropriate chapters, will guide you back to peak form.

After you've mastered the physical skills, you'll want to consider learning how to use your bike for cardiovascular fitness, go on long trips, or enjoy off-road recreation activities. For these, there is a special chapter, Going Beyond: Possibilities for the Future.

At the back of the book, you'll find information on establishing your own exercise program for peak fitness as well as gearing information to aid you in purchasing the bicycle best for your needs.

Cycling—a sport for life!

Scott, Foresman and Company   18357